TRUMP SUIT HEADACHES

Rx: For Declarers And Defenders

PRESCRIBED BY:

JAMES MARSH STERNBERG MD (DR. J)

authorHOUSE

AuthorHouse™
1663 Liberty Drive
Bloomington, IN 47403
www.authorhouse.com
Phone: 833-262-8899

Published by AuthorHouse 10/12/2023

ISBN: 978-1-6655-1073-8 (sc)
ISBN: 978-1-6655-1072-1 (e)

Library of Congress Control Number: 2020924607

Print information available on the last page.

Any people depicted in stock imagery provided by Getty Images are models,
and such images are being used for illustrative purposes only.
Certain stock imagery © Getty Images.

This book is printed on acid-free paper.

Also by James Marsh Sternberg

Playing to Trick One – No Mulligans in Bridge (2nd Ed)

Trump Suit Headaches; Rx for Declarers and Defenders (2nd Ed)

The Finesse; Only a Last Resort

Blocking and Unblocking

Shortness – a Key to Better Bidding (2nd Ed)

When Michaels Met The Unusual

From Zero to Three Hundred; A Bridge Journey

Reversing the Dummy

Trump Promotion; The Uppercut

Active or Passive – Becoming a Better Defender

To Ruff or Not to Ruff, That is the Question

Also by James Marsh Sternberg

I, Radiologist; The Evolution of Medicine in 'West' West Broward County

By James Marsh Sternberg with Danny Kleinman

Second Hand High; Third Hand Not So High

An Entry, An Entry, My Kingdom For An Entry

L O L; Loser on Loser

In Search of a Second Suit

Elimination and Endplay

Suit Preference; Abused and Misused

Solving the Mystery of the Redouble

THIS BOOK IS DEDICATED TO

THE MEMORY OF

MY DAUGHTER

SANDRA CAREY STERNBERG

CONTENTS

ACKNOWLEDGMENTS

This book would not have been possible without the help of several friends. Frank Stewart, Michael Lawrence, Anne Lund, Marty Bergen and Eddie Kantar all kindly provided suggestions for material for the book.

I am forever indebted to Hall of Famer Fred Hamilton and the late Bernie Chazen, without whose guidance and teaching I could not have achieved whatever success I have had in bridge.

Special thanks to my editor Randy Baron, the best bridge editor one could be so fortunate to be associated with.

And to Vickie Lee Bader, whose love and patience helped guide me thru the many hours of this endeavor.

James Marsh Sternberg MD
Palm Beach Gardens, FL
mmay001@aol.com

PRELUDE

'Headaches' was first published three years ago, December 2020. It was my second book in what has become a series of seventeen books on selected topics in bridge. With 228 quiz deals, it is my largest book.

When 'Headaches' was written, my career as a writer was in it's infancy. I felt I could significantly improve many of the deals as well as add some fresh material.

Three years and seventeen books have taught me a lot. Co-authoring some of them with Danny Kleinman has been very helpful in improving my writing skills. The reviews of the first edition in various bridge magazines have also given me suggestions which have been incorporated into the second edition. Hopefully, any typos in the first edition have been corrected. I hope you enjoy the deals.

James Marsh Sternberg, MD (Dr J)   October, 2023
Palm Beach Gardens, FL

INTRODUCTION

The trump suit adds a dimension that makes bridge so different from other card games. In a suit contract, play is complicated by declarer's need to keep control. If control is lost, it may be almost impossible to make proper use of one's strength in the side suits.

Before playing to Trick 1, one should ask what might go wrong? If playing a suit contract, is there a reason not to draw trumps? Or maybe just some of the trumps?

Safety plays apply to all suits. Focus is on the trump suit, but the same general principles can be applied elsewhere. The skillful player displays pessimism. Suits will break badly, all finesses will lose, that's the starting point, and things will probably get worse.

We will look at a series of hands both from the declarer's perspective and the defenders', with focus on the trumps, and see how some of these problems might be managed. With bad trump splits, or playing 4/3 or 5/2 fits, it's easy to lose control. Timing is crucial.

On defense, we will look at trump promotion, shortening declarer's trump holding, the importance of the ace of trumps, when to ruff, when not to ruff, falsecarding, and other weapons available.

Some years ago, an expert friend of mine was in the hospital for a surgical procedure. He had left my number as a contact. A nurse called me from the recovery room. She said "Your friend isn't fully awake yet, but he's yelling something about 'the darn trumps are always 4/1' and I don't know what do for him." "Give him a better trump split, he will be just fine," I suggested. I could almost see the quizzical look on her face as she hung up.

In the declarer sections, the East-West hands are shown for convenience. I suggest you cover them when studying the deal On defense, often only your hand and the dummy are shown at the top of the page while others show all four hands.

Assume IMP or rubber bridge scoring. Forget about overtricks; just try to make or break the contracts.

MISSING

HIGH

HONORS

HIGH HONOR PROBLEMS

♠ Q J 4 3 2

♠ A 10 8 7 5

Declarer is in a contract, any contract and this is the trump suit. Actually, it could be any suit.

So how should you play if you cannot afford to lose a trick? Your options obviously are to finesse or not to finesse.

You are in the dummy and when you lead the queen, your right hand opponent follows with a low card.

There has been no bidding or anything in the play to tell you the king is on your left. Should you go up ace?

Here are the possible layouts after RHO has followed:

K	9 6
6	K 9
9	K 6
---	K 9 6

So in only one of four situations is it right to play the ace. LHO is just as likely to have the singleton 6 or 9. The king will drop less than 15% of the time.

MORE HIGH HONOR PROBLEMS

♠ J 10 9

♠ A K 4 3 2

Spades are trumps.

Another handling problem. You are going to lose enough tricks so that you cannot afford to lose a trump trick.

But right now you have plenty of entries. Should you play the ace first, then go to dummy to take a finesse or take a first round finesse? You are not going to cash the A-K, that is an anti-percentage play. For once, eight ever, nine never.

To make your contract, you need your right hand opponent to have the queen or left hand opponent a singleton queen.
If trumps are 3/2, it doesn't matter what you do. But what if they are 4/1?

LHO can have a singleton queen, eight, seven, six, or five.

If it's the queen, playing the ace is good, very good. But in the other four situations, it will cost you a trick. Right hand opponent will cover the second card and promote a trick for herself.

So if the trumps are 4/1, go with the 80% play, a first round finesse. Lead the jack and keep repeating the finesse.

DRAW TRUMPS: MISSING HIGH HONORS

♠ A Q 7 5

♠ 10 9 8 6 3

Contract: 6 ♠

You have no outside losers, but here is your trump suit. What's your play?

Here are your three choices: 1) Low to the queen. 2) Lead the ten. 3) Other.

If you need all the tricks, low to the queen is best, but you are in six spades, not seven. Number three, other, leading to the ace is best. Why?

If you lead to the queen and your right hand opponent East wins, you won't know on the next round whether you should finesse for the jack or cash the ace.

If you lead the ten and lose to East's jack, same problem.

After cashing the ace when East follows small, lead towards the queen. As long as West did not start with a void or small singleton, in which case you were never making, you will take twelve tricks. If you drop the jack from either opponent under the ace, you will lose just one trick.

If West has played his singleton king, East will win one trick. If you drop the singleton king from East, finesse West for the jack.

Slams are high paying contracts. This safety play should be high on your priority list, not worrying about overtricks.

TRYING TO CRASH THE TOP HONORS

♠ K Q 10
♥ Q 6 4
♦ K 7 6 4 3
♣ 9 2

♠ A J
♥ J 10 9 8 7 5 2
♦ A
♣ Q J 10

Contract: 4 ♥
Opening Lead: ♣ Ace

A little unlucky. A little overbidding. Anyhow, is there any hope for this contract after the opponents take the first two club tricks?

Give up or what?

The situation is grim but not hopeless. But play with confidence. Only you know you are in trouble. But you need a little help from the opponents assuming the A-K are not in the same hand but something like K3 and singleton Ace.

Two choices. You could lead the queen from dummy and hope East covers with K3. Or you could lead low towards the queen hoping a nervous West with K3 jumps up. Any ideas?

Yes. If possible, try to judge your opponents and put pressure on whoever you judge to be the weaker of the two. If you think it's West, lead towards the queen. If you think it's East, lead the queen. Try to make the weaker player find the wrong play, not the strong one.

Will this work? It doesn't matter. Try to give yourself a chance. Don't just give up. And if it works, enjoy the yelling and screaming that follows.

DRAWING TRUMPS MISSING HONORS

♠ 6

♠? (?)   ♠ ? (?)

♠ K J 10 9 7 4 3

Here you are again. You started with two trumps in dummy, but had to ruff once.

So this is it, your one chance to lead towards your hand missing four to the A-Q-x-x.

You can afford to lose one trump trick, not two. West does not have A-Q or this would not be in the book.

If the missing four are split 2/2, toss a coin. But South can't gain by finessing the jack. If East has Q-x-x or A-Q-x, he will always lose two tricks.

South should put up the king. His play is significant only if West has a singleton queen.

DEAL 1   MISSING SOME HIGH HONORS

♠ 4
♥ K 3
♦ Q 8 3 2
♣ Q 10 9 8 6 3

♠ K Q 8 7 6 3 2
♥ Q 5
♦ A K
♣ A K

Contract: 4 ♠
Opening Lead: ♦ Jack

Declarer has one loser outside the trump suit. So he has to bring in the spades for only two losers. He led the ♠K, losing to East's ace and another diamond came back. Next he led the ♠Q and East showed out.

West's ♠109 meant down one.

Any ideas on how to handle the suit? Find a partner with more trumps?

If the trumps are 3/2 nothing much matters. The only real problem is 4/1 with a defender having a singleton ace. So start with a low trump.

If a defender wins the first trick cheaply, later lead the king and hope for a 3/2 split. Good days, bad days.

West's ♠'s   J 10 9 5
East's ♠'s   Ace

DEAL 2   CARD COMBINATIONS

♠ 10 7 6 5
♥ 2
♦ 8 5 4 3
♣ J 6 4 2

♠ A K
♥ K Q 10 9 8 6 4
♦ A K 6
♣ K

Contract: 4 ♥
Opening Lead: ♦ Queen

South has two outside losers, so he needs to hold his trump losers to one. Playing for a singleton ♥A won't help because that would leave the other defender with ♥J75.

Declarer led the ♥K and both opponents followed low. She continued with a low trump.

Was this the right play? Or should she have played the ♥Q?

It depends on the level of the opponents. You should lead the ♥Q next, not low. Why?

A good defender holding ♥Ax (partner ♥Jxx) would know if he did not capture the king, declarer might lead a small trump next dropping his ace. With ♥Axx, he would duck to give you a chance to go wrong. Because if he wins his ace, declarer has no choice on the next round but to play the queen, which now captures the jack.

West holding ♥Axx played in a way to give South a guess. In some cases South will do the wrong thing.

DEAL 3 TRUMP CARD COMBINATIONS

♠ K 8 7 6 2
♥ ----
♦ K Q J 2
♣ K 6 5 2

♠ ----
♥ A J 10 6 5 4 2
♦ A 8 7
♣ Q J 10

Contract: 4 ♥
Opening Lead: ♣ 9

East won the opening lead and returned a low spade which South ruffed. Needing to hold his trump losers to two, he led the ♥A, then the ♥J.

Was this the right play? Why?

South does not have enough spot cards so that he can throw them around like confetti. The winning play is to lead the ♥A, then a small one. Why?

If the suit is 3/3, the bellboy can make this hand. If the suit is 4/2 with both honors in the hand with four, ♥KQxx opposite ♥xx, the bellboy is going down no matter what.

But if the 4/2 split is ♥Kx or ♥Qx opposite ♥xxxx, then ace and a small one lets you lose to the now bare honor and pick up the last two little cards with the ♥ J 10.

DEAL 4 MISSING THE HIGH HONORS

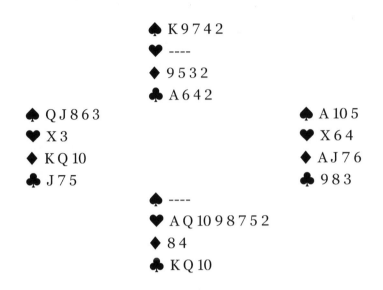

♠ K 9 7 4 2
♥ ----
♦ 9 5 3 2
♣ A 6 4 2

♠ Q J 8 6 3
♥ X 3
♦ K Q 10
♣ J 7 5

♠ A 10 5
♥ X 6 4
♦ A J 7 6
♣ 9 8 3

♠ ----
♥ A Q 10 9 8 7 5 2
♦ 8 4
♣ K Q 10

East	South	West	North
1 ♦	4 ♥	Dbl	All Pass

Opening Lead:　♦ King

West led the ♦KQ, then the ♦10. South ruffed the third round and needed to hold the heart losers to one. What does he need in hearts?

Either ♥Jx, Kx, or a singleton honor. He played the ♥A, both defenders followed small. Now he had to choose, low (for Kx) or queen (for Jx). He played the_____, down one.

Which are you going to choose? What is your thinking?

East opened the bidding and West has shown up with the ♦KQ. So East likely has the ♥K. But if he has K x and declarer now plays a low one, East will play another diamond and West will score his jack on a trump promotion.

No good. So play for ♥Jx in West, ♥Kxx in East, and lead the ♥Q.

DEAL 5   MORE MISSING HIGH HONORS

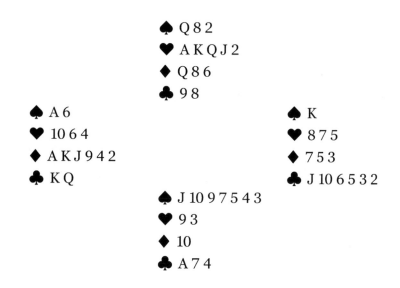

♠ Q 8 2
♥ A K Q J 2
♦ Q 8 6
♣ 9 8

♠ A 6
♥ 10 6 4
♦ A K J 9 4 2
♣ K Q

♠ K
♥ 8 7 5
♦ 7 5 3
♣ J 10 6 5 3 2

♠ J 10 9 7 5 4 3
♥ 9 3
♦ 10
♣ A 7 4

West	North	East	South
1 ♦	1 ♥	P	1 ♠
3 ♦	3 ♠	P	4 ♠
All Pass			

Opening Lead: ♦ Ace

West leads the ♦A and switches to the ♣K and declarer's ace.

Looking at four losers, declarer tried a play we discussed earlier. Lead towards dummy; maybe West has K x and there will be an "accident". Good idea, but down one.

Any other ideas without resorting to a defensive error?

Maybe, if hearts are 3/3. Play the ♥AKQ discarding a club. Now lead the ♥J, discarding your last club.

If East ruffs, that was a trick he was going to get anyhow. If West ruffs with the ♥six, there will be a big crash of the high honors later. Worth a try.

DEAL 6   MISSING TOP HONORS

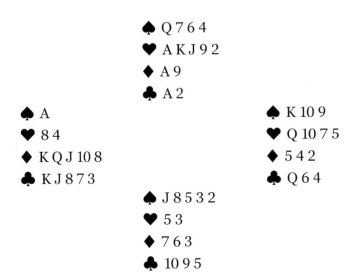

North	East	South	West
1 ♥	P	P	2 ♦
Dbl	P	2 ♠	3 ♣
3 ♠		All Pass	

Opening Lead: ♦ King

Declarer had two losers in the minors, so he needed to hold his trump losers to two. This kind of hand makes you appreciate 10's and 9's.

He played a low spade to the ♠J, losing to the ♠A and lost two more spades to East. Down one.

How would you have played the spade suit and why?

Spades are not 4/0. Only East could have four and with ♠AK109 would certainly have doubled. If spades are 2/2 nothing matters.

So play West for a singleton honor, either by playing low from both hands, or lead the ♠Q, then later towards the ♠J.

Anything but by starting low to the ♠J.

DEAL 7   HIGH TRUMP HEADACHES

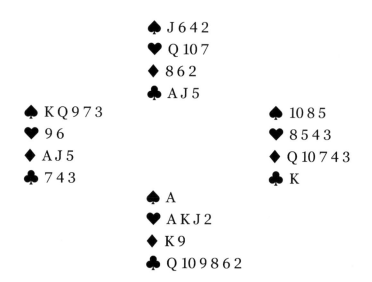

♠ J 6 4 2
♥ Q 10 7
♦ 8 6 2
♣ A J 5

♠ K Q 9 7 3   ♠ 10 8 5
♥ 9 6   ♥ 8 5 4 3
♦ A J 5   ♦ Q 10 7 4 3
♣ 7 4 3   ♣ K

♠ A
♥ A K J 2
♦ K 9
♣ Q 10 9 8 6 2

West	North	East	South
P	P	P	1 ♣
1 ♠	1NT	P	2 ♥
P	3 ♣	P	5 ♣
	All Pass		

Opening Lead: ♠ King

At one table, declarer won the opening lead and took a club finesse. East won the ♣K and returned a low diamond. South lost two diamond tricks. Down one.

Declarer's line of play was never making five clubs. Why?

Both opponents are passed hands. West has, we assume, the ♠KQ. If West has the ♣K, East will have the ♦A because West is a passed hand.

But if West has the ♦A, East must have the ♣K. Declarer must guard against a singleton ♣K by leading to the ♣A.

DEAL 8   MORE HEADACHES

♠ A 7 2
♥ K J 9 2
♦ 10 9 8 4 3
♣ 9

♠ 3
♥ A Q 5
♦ K J 7 6 5
♣ A K Q 8

South	North
1 ♦	1 ♥
3 ♣	4 ♦
4 NT	5 ♣
6 ♦	P

Opening Lead: ♠ King

You are in a good contract, but you have to guess the ace and queen of the trump suit. Of course, there may be no guess; if either defender has ♦AQ2, you are going down.

At the first table, the declarer led low from dummy, East played the two (of course, big help), and declarer played_____? Down one.

What would you play and why?

There is no perfect answer. But assuming the ace and queen are split, think about the bidding, or more importantly, the lack of bidding.

West led the ♠K. So assume he has ♠KQxxx. If you were West with that spade holding and a side ace, might you not have taken your life in your hands and overcalled one spade?

Not much to go on, granted, but if I had to guess, I think East has the ♦A. So I would go up with the ♦K.

The E/W hands? Whatever you like. It's the thought process that is important.

14

DEAL 9   DEVIOUS

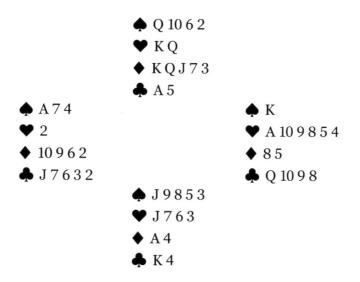

♠ Q 10 6 2
♥ K Q
♦ K Q J 7 3
♣ A 5

♠ A 7 4
♥ 2
♦ 10 9 6 2
♣ J 7 6 3 2

♠ K
♥ A 10 9 8 5 4
♦ 8 5
♣ Q 10 9 8

♠ J 9 8 5 3
♥ J 7 6 3
♦ A 4
♣ K 4

North	East	South	West
1 ♦	1 ♥	1 ♠	P
3 ♠	P	4 ♠	All Pass

Opening Lead: ♥ 2

At the first table, East won the opening lead and gave West a heart ruff. Declarer won the club return but lost two more trump tricks.

Down one.

Despite four losers, do you see any way to bring this contract home?

At the other table, the declarer was a little more devious. After the same start, she won the club return with the ♣A and came to her hand with the ♦A.

Now she led the good ♥J, looking like she wanted to discard a club loser. Well, I don't have to tell you what happened.

West said "Oh no you don't," and ruffed. Declared said "Thank you very much" and overruffed. The loud crash on the next trick was heard in the next room.

Making four spades.

15

DEAL 10   MORE ASPIRIN, PLEASE

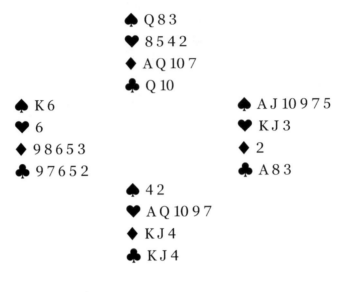

```
              ♠ Q 8 3
              ♥ 8 5 4 2
              ♦ A Q 10 7
              ♣ Q 10
  ♠ K 6                      ♠ A J 10 9 7 5
  ♥ 6                        ♥ K J 3
  ♦ 9 8 6 5 3                ♦ 2
  ♣ 9 7 6 5 2                ♣ A 8 3
              ♠ 4 2
              ♥ A Q 10 9 7
              ♦ K J 4
              ♣ K J 4
```

South	West	North	East
1 ♥	P	3 ♥	3 ♠
4 ♥	All Pass		

Opening Lead: ♠ King

At the first table West led the spade king, then the six to East's nine. East cashed the club ace and played another club. Declarer needed to pick up the trump suit for no losers. The normal play is low to the queen, then cash the ace.

Declarer won the second club in dummy and led a heart. East played the three, declarer the queen, West the six. But when declarer played the heart ace, West showed out. Down one.

Unlucky, misplayed, what do you think? Running out of aspirin?

One question you might ask yourself is who was East? What would most East players do at Trick 3? Sure, try to give West a spade ruff. So why didn't he?

The missing trump honors are the king and the jack. But when West can't overruff, you will know East has both of them.

Nice play by East, not giving the show away. But declarer should pick up on that inference too and take a double finesse.

DEAL 11　CAN YOU UP THE ODDS?

♠ 7 2
♥ 2
♦ K Q 6 3
♣ A J 9 8 7 5

♠ A 6 5 3
♥ A Q 8 3
♦ 4
♣ Q 10 6 4

Contract:　5 ♣
Opening Lead:　♠ Queen

West led the queen of spades, attacking South's weakness. With a sure diamond loser and a spade loser, declarer had to consider the trump suit missing three to the king. The odds favor taking a finesse, so he did.

Was this the correct play?

It's good to know some percentages but you have to look at the entire hand, not just focus on what might be only a part of the problem (or the solution).

Try to increase the odds a bit. There is another possible finesse. Do you see it?

If you take a heart finesse and it wins, no more spade loser. So try to combine your chances. On a good day the trump king will be singleton offside (about 13%).

First try leading the club queen. Who knows, someone might cover, but in any case, go up with the ace. If nothing good happens, take the heart finesse.

This increases your chances significantly. True, you may go down an extra trick, but it's worth the effort. You have upped the odds of making five clubs.

The E/W hands? Not important. Make them any way you like.

17

DEAL 12 A HEADACHE WITH A MIRACLE CURE

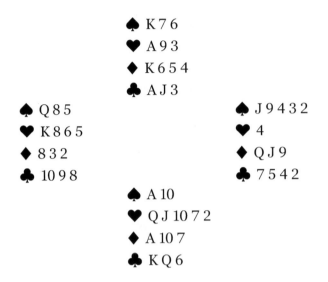

♠ K 7 6
♥ A 9 3
♦ K 6 5 4
♣ A J 3

♠ Q 8 5
♥ K 8 6 5
♦ 8 3 2
♣ 10 9 8

♠ J 9 4 3 2
♥ 4
♦ Q J 9
♣ 7 5 4 2

♠ A 10
♥ Q J 10 7 2
♦ A 10 7
♣ K Q 6

Contract: 6 ♥
Opening Lead: ♣ 10

This is a hand Mike Lawrence showed some years ago. No matter how bad your headache, there is a cure. It shows why you should never give up.

You have a diamond loser. At Trick 2, you lead the heart queen, it wins. You lead a heart to the nine, it wins but East shows out.

North now has singleton ♥ A, West has ♥ K 8, with still a diamond to lose. Are you down? Probably, but picture an ending shown below with East on lead.

Cash three rounds of clubs. Cash the A-K of spades and ruff a spade. Now three rounds of diamonds. If East has to win the third round, with, for example, Q J x, or if he did not unblock the queen, your wish has come true.

In the 2-card ending, any card East plays, you ruff with the heart ten.

North: ♥ A ♦ 4

West: ♥ K 8   East   Immaterial

South: ♥ J 10

If West overruffs, North plays the ace. If West underruffs, North plays the diamond. Can you imagine West's frustration? After the third trick, he wanted to claim you were down one. Special thanks to Mike Lawrence for this one.

18

DEAL 13 TRANSPORTATION

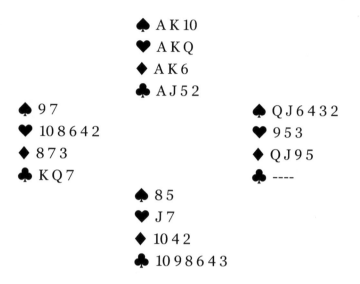

♠ A K 10
♥ A K Q
♦ A K 6
♣ A J 5 2

♠ 9 7
♥ 10 8 6 4 2
♦ 8 7 3
♣ K Q 7

♠ Q J 6 4 3 2
♥ 9 5 3
♦ Q J 9 5
♣ ----

♠ 8 5
♥ J 7
♦ 10 4 2
♣ 10 9 8 6 4 3

Contract: 6 ♣

Opening Lead: ♥ 4

Declarer asked herself what could go wrong? The only worry is a bad trump break. If East has ♣ K Q 7, no play. So to cater to West having all three, she did well to start low from both hands. East discarded a spade, West won and returned a diamond.

OK, now she had to get back to her hand to finesse the club. She played the A-K of spades and ruffed a spade. West overruffed. Down one.

After such a good start, what's the best way back to the South hand?

East's discard suggests length. Cash the high hearts, discarding one spade. Now spade ace, ruff a spade, club finesse.

The diamond loser can go on the other high spade later.

DEAL 14   YES OR NO?

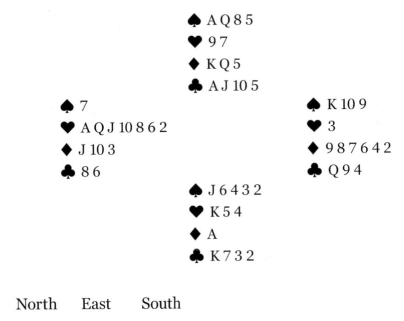

♠ A Q 8 5
♥ 9 7
♦ K Q 5
♣ A J 10 5

♠ 7
♥ A Q J 10 8 6 2
♦ J 10 3
♣ 8 6

♠ K 10 9
♥ 3
♦ 9 8 7 6 4 2
♣ Q 9 4

♠ J 6 4 3 2
♥ K 5 4
♦ A
♣ K 7 3 2

West	North	East	South
3 ♥	Dbl	P	4 ♠
	All Pass		

Opening Lead: ♦ Jack

Declarer won the opening lead in hand and led the spade two to the queen and king. East returned his heart. West won two heart tricks and played a third heart.

Now what? East had a trump trick coming, no matter what South did. Down one.

Is there a rule that says you have to take every finesse you see?

Were you shocked the spade finesse lost? Wow, what a surprise! To avoid this mess, the other declarer played a spade to the ace, then led a low spade from dummy. What could East do?

He took his king and the defense took two hearts. But now declarer had a high trump in dummy to ruff the last heart. And two small clubs went on the K-Q of diamonds.

Making four spades, no finesses.

DEAL 15   PLAY FOR WHAT YOU NEED

$$\spadesuit \text{ A } 10\ 8\ 4$$
$$\heartsuit \text{ J } 9\ 8$$
$$\diamondsuit \text{ K J } 10$$
$$\clubsuit \text{ K Q } 7$$

$$\spadesuit \text{ Q } 6\ 5\ 3\ 2$$
$$\heartsuit \text{ K Q } 10$$
$$\diamondsuit \text{ A Q } 2$$
$$\clubsuit \text{ A J}$$

Contract: 6 ♠
Opening Lead: ♦ 9

A problem of quality but not quantity. With a sure heart loser, declarer can't afford a trump loser. One declarer played the trump ace hoping to drop a singleton king.

But that served no purpose for even if successful, would leave the other defender with J-9, a sure trick.

Is there any hope for this contract?

When skies look cloudy and grey, try to find a ray of sunshine. If there is even one lie of the cards that would work, play for that. Is there one here?

If West has ♠ K97 and East ♠ J, by leading the queen, the defense has no answer. Win the opening lead in hand and lead the spade queen. If West covers, the jack gets smothered and you can return to hand to finesse against the nine.

If West ducks, he ducks.

DEAL 16   SELF PROTECTION

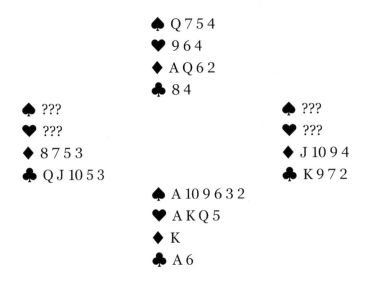

♠ Q 7 5 4
♥ 9 6 4
♦ A Q 6 2
♣ 8 4

♠ ???
♥ ???
♦ 8 7 5 3
♣ Q J 10 5 3

♠ ???
♥ ???
♦ J 10 9 4
♣ K 9 7 2

♠ A 10 9 6 3 2
♥ A K Q 5
♦ K
♣ A 6

Contract: 6 ♠
Opening Lead: ♣ Queen

Declarer won the club ace. She played the diamond king to dummy's ace and discarded her club loser on the diamond queen.

OK, time to face the trump problem. She decided to lead a low spade to the ace, then low towards dummy. So it went 4, 8, ace, _____.

What do you think of declarer's plan?

The main problem is to protect yourself against a 3/0 break. You have a 100% safety play. Lead low from dummy and if East follows, just cover whatever card he plays. If West follows, winning or not, the problem is over.

And if East shows out, win the ace and lead towards the queen. Either way you cannot lose more than one spade trick.

East's spades: ♠ K J 8
West's spades: ♠ ----

DEAL 17   LISTEN TO THE BIDDING

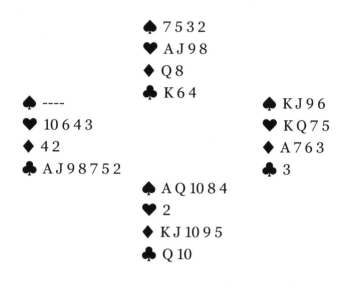

♠ 7 5 3 2
♥ A J 9 8
♦ Q 8
♣ K 6 4

♠ ----
♥ 10 6 4 3
♦ 4 2
♣ A J 9 8 7 5 2

♠ K J 9 6
♥ K Q 7 5
♦ A 7 6 3
♣ 3

♠ A Q 10 8 4
♥ 2
♦ K J 10 9 5
♣ Q 10

East	South	West	North
1 ♦	1 ♠	Dbl	2 ♦
P	4 ♠	All Pass	

Opening Lead: ♦ 4

East won the diamond ace and returned a small club. West won the ace and returned a small club, East ruffing with the spade six. East returned a small diamond, West following with the two.

Having lost three tricks, declarer needed to pick up the trump suit for no losers. He went to dummy and led a small spade, East played the nine.

Declarer played the _____, down one.

How would you have played the trumps?

The answer is in the bidding. Can you figure out the distribution? How many minor suit cards does East, the opening bidder, have? He opened one diamond and has four (West showed two) plus a singleton club.

His shape must be 4=4=4=1. West is void in spades. East started with ♠KJ96. West probably could have made a better bid of three preemptive clubs instead of a negative double.

DEAL 18   MORE MISSING HIGH HONORS

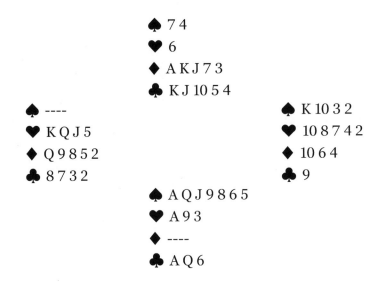

♠ 7 4
♥ 6
♦ A K J 7 3
♣ K J 10 5 4

♠ ----
♥ K Q J 5
♦ Q 9 8 5 2
♣ 8 7 3 2

♠ K 10 3 2
♥ 10 8 7 4 2
♦ 10 6 4
♣ 9

♠ A Q J 9 8 6 5
♥ A 9 3
♦ ----
♣ A Q 6

Contract: 6 ♠
Opening Lead: ♥ King

One declarer won the heart ace, ruffed a heart, and discarded his last heart on the diamond ace. He then led a spade to the queen.

When West showed out, he lost two trump tricks, down one. When comparing with his teammates, found the opponents had made six spades.

How did the other declarer make twelve tricks?

You can't be too careful. At Trick 2, cash the spade ace. If both defenders follow, ruff a heart, discard a heart, ruff a diamond and lead the spade queen.

When West shows out, lead a club to dummy, discard two hearts on the A-K of diamonds and lead a spade. Twelve tricks, what's the problem?

DEAL 19 ANOTHER TRUMP KING PROBLEM

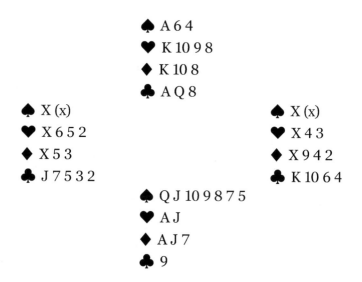

Contract: 6 ♠

Opening Lead: ♣ 3

So many finesses, where to start? (Yes, West might have 14 cards). At the first table, declarer won the club ace, ruffed a club, and took a losing trump finesse. He later misguessed the heart queen, down one.

Unlucky or misplayed?

Why are you taking any finesses? Just because you can? The way to assure this contract is to take no finesses.

Win the opening lead and ruff a club. Cash the trump ace and ruff another club. Play a trump. Game, set, and match.

Whoever wins the trump king has to lead a red suit, guessing that queen for you, or lead a club, conceding a ruff/sluff.

Finesses are useful, but experts use them only as a last resort.

DEAL 20   TIMING

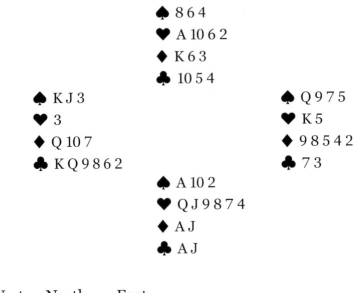

♠ 8 6 4
♥ A 10 6 2
♦ K 6 3
♣ 10 5 4

♠ K J 3
♥ 3
♦ Q 10 7
♣ K Q 9 8 6 2

♠ Q 9 7 5
♥ K 5
♦ 9 8 5 4 2
♣ 7 3

♠ A 10 2
♥ Q J 9 8 7 4
♦ A J
♣ A J

South	West	North	East
1 ♥	2 ♣	2 ♥	P
4 ♥		All Pass	

Opening Lead: ♣ King

At the first table, declarer, relieved he did not receive a spade lead, won the opening lead and took a trump finesse. East won and returned a club.

West continued clubs, East ruffing. Declarer overruffed but he still had two spade losers. Down one.

Unlucky (as usual, moaned South) or mistimed?

At the other table, the declarer timed the hand better. When he led the trump queen and West did not cover, he played the ace of hearts. Then he played a second club.

Now he was one step ahead in the race. If East ruffed a club return, declarer could throw a loser, a loser-on-loser play. If they switched to spades, his club ten was good for a spade discard. Ten tricks.

SAFETY

PLAYS

DEAL 21   BASIC SAFETY PLAY

♠ K 7
♥ K J 5 2
♦ A K Q 7
♣ K 6 5

♠ 8 2
♥ A 9 7 6 4
♦ J 10 6
♣ A J 7

Contract: 4 ♥
Opening Lead: ♠ Queen

Declarer loses the first two tricks. The contract is safe as long as declarer doesn't lose two heart tricks. If hearts are 2/2, declarer has the rest. If they are 3/1, there is a likely heart loser.

OK, but what if you are having a bad day and the trumps are 4/0? You have some work to do. How should you tackle the trumps when you get in at Trick 3? Does it matter how you start?

Is there a way to overcome a 4/0 break in either hand?

Leading the ace ♥A would be OK if West has four, but bad if East has ♥Q1083. By leading low to the king first, you can handle 4/0 in either hand.

When West shows out, you lead from dummy. East must play the ten, South the ace and East is limited to one trick.

If East shows out on the king, play back to your ace and lead towards the jack, holding West to one trick.

DEAL 22   TRUMP SAFETY PLAY

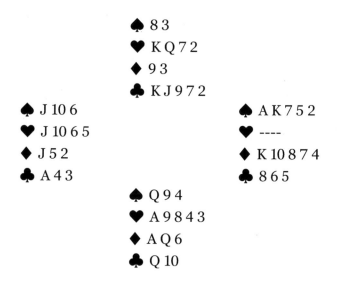

```
                    ♠ 8 3
                    ♥ K Q 7 2
                    ♦ 9 3
                    ♣ K J 9 7 2
    ♠ J 10 6                       ♠ A K 7 5 2
    ♥ J 10 6 5                     ♥ ----
    ♦ J 5 2                        ♦ K 10 8 7 4
    ♣ A 4 3                        ♣ 8 6 5
                    ♠ Q 9 4
                    ♥ A 9 8 4 3
                    ♦ A Q 6
                    ♣ Q 10
```

Contract: 4 ♥

Opening Lead: ♠ Jack

East won the opening lead, declarer falsecarding with the nine. If East thinks declarer started with ♠Q9 doubleton and cashes the ace, then declarer won't have to worry about the diamond finesse.

But East switches to a low diamond. The finesse wins. OK, but now the trumps. Declarer led low to the ♥K. East showed out.

Down one. Sad.

What is the basic safety play in this typical situation?

If East has four trumps to the ♥J1065, you must lose a trick. But if West has them, you can survive by starting with the ace. East shows out, so you lead a heart to the ten and queen.

Start setting up the clubs to get back to your hand for another trump finesse.

DEAL 23   SAFETY PLAY? DEPENDS ON THE GAME

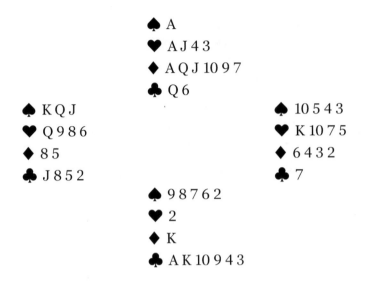

♠ A
♥ A J 4 3
♦ A Q J 10 9 7
♣ Q 6

♠ K Q J
♥ Q 9 8 6
♦ 8 5
♣ J 8 5 2

♠ 10 5 4 3
♥ K 10 7 5
♦ 6 4 3 2
♣ 7

♠ 9 8 7 6 2
♥ 2
♦ K
♣ A K 10 9 4 3

Contract: 6 ♣

Opening Lead: ♠ King

This looked like a no-brainer if trumps were 3/2. Declarer won the opening lead, cashed the club queen and led a club. East showed out.

Ouch! Can't run the diamonds with a trump out and can't knock out the trump jack without losing a bunch of spades.

Should declarer have taken a safety play of queen, then low to the ten?

It's not clear. At matchpoints it's nip and tuck to give up on a likely overtrick. If you think just being in a slam will be a good score, or at IMP's, take the safety play by all means.

At matchpoints if you think most of the field will be in 6C or 6D, you can't afford to play safe for six, because 70% of the time those contracts will make seven.

DEAL 24 SAFETY PLAY OR NOT?

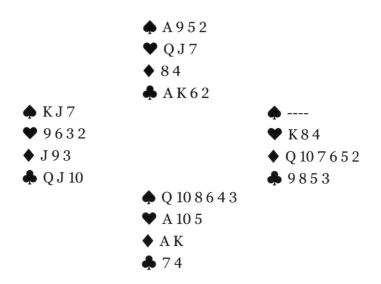

♠ A 9 5 2
♥ Q J 7
♦ 8 4
♣ A K 6 2

♠ K J 7　　　　　　　　♠ ----
♥ 9 6 3 2　　　　　　　♥ K 8 4
♦ J 9 3　　　　　　　　♦ Q 10 7 6 5 2
♣ Q J 10　　　　　　　♣ 9 8 5 3

♠ Q 10 8 6 4 3
♥ A 10 5
♦ A K
♣ 7 4

Contract: 6 ♠

Opening Lead: ♣ Queen

In a team game, declarer won the opening lead. He played the ace of trumps and East showed out. West now had two trump tricks. The heart finesse was just a matter of how many undertricks. When comparing with his teammates, he asked "How many did they go down?" "We were -980" was the reply. Painful.

What happened at the other table? Bad defense? Not possible.

The question is how to play the trump suit, but declarer needs more information. He is not ready; he needs to know if the heart finesse will win or lose. Then he knows if he can make a safety play in trumps.

When the heart finesse wins, declarer can take the safety play of coming to hand with a diamond and leading a spade, intending to play the nine if West plays the seven.

If he cannot afford to lose a trump, then cashing the ace is the only option.

DEAL 25   TRUMP SAFETY PLAY

♠ A
♥ A J 9 5 3
♦ Q J 7 3
♣ A Q 2

♠ K Q J
♥ 10
♦ A 6 4 2
♣ K J 10 5 3

Contract: 6 ♦
Opening Lead: ♠ 10

A good slam, certainly better than 6 NT. If diamonds are 3/2, slam will be cold. One declarer led the diamond queen, losing to the king.

When East showed up with the ♦10985, the contract was down one.

What should declarer have been thinking about?

Always ask: What can go wrong and what can I do about it? Declarer can handle some, but not all 4/1 breaks. If either defender has a singleton king, starting with the ace is good, losing one trick later.

If West has a singleton and East has four to the king, you are going down. But if West has four to the king, starting with the ace and leading to dummy will hold him to one trick.

West's ♦'s   K
East's ♦'s   10 9 8 5

DEAL 26   WHO IS IT?

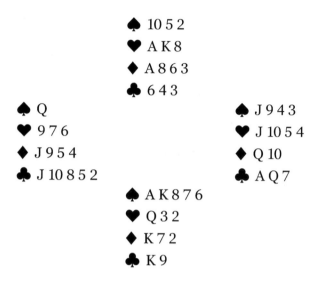

♠ 10 5 2
♥ A K 8
♦ A 8 6 3
♣ 6 4 3

♠ Q
♥ 9 7 6
♦ J 9 5 4
♣ J 10 8 5 2

♠ J 9 4 3
♥ J 10 5 4
♦ Q 10
♣ A Q 7

♠ A K 8 7 6
♥ Q 3 2
♦ K 7 2
♣ K 9

Contract: 4 ♠
Opening Lead: ♣ Jack

OK, the club ace was onside and you have a diamond loser. You will make four spades if you can hold your trump losers to one. You lay down the spade ace and LHO plays the queen. Now what?

First look over and see who West is. If it's your grandmother, that's a singleton queen. But nope, it's Fred Hamilton, looking back at you. Great.

Do you lay down the king? If East started with ♠J943, you will go down.

Leading the king even against Freddie is probably an invitation to disaster when there is a safety play to guarantee your contract.

Lead a low spade to the ten and East's jack. Later you can finesse East out of his remaining ♠94.

DEAL 27   MIKE SAYS

♠ A K Q 5 4 3
♥ 9
♦ A J
♣ Q J 5 4

♠ 2
♥ A Q 6 3
♦ K Q 4
♣ A 9 6 3 2

Contract: 6 ♣
Opening Lead: ♥ Jack

Reaching six clubs is fine. But as Mike Lawrence says, "They don't pay you for bidding it. They pay you for making it." And as usual, ask yourself what can go wrong.

Plenty of tricks outside the trump suit, just can't afford to lose two club tricks. And of course. the trumps are 4/1.

If East has ♣K1087, you will lose two by starting with the ace.

If West has ♣K1087, you will lose two if you lead the queen.

What's it going to be, Alfie? There is a 100% play.

Lead a low club from your hand to start. If West has all four and ducks, come back and do it again.

If East has all four, he will win his king and you can later finesse against his ten.

34

DEAL 28   WHAT CAN GO WRONG?

♠ J 7 6 4
♥ K Q 6
♦ K Q 7 2
♣ 9 3

♠ A K 8 5 3
♥ A 2
♦ A J 4 3
♣ A 10

Contract: 6 ♠
Opening Lead: ♥ Jack

Pretty good grand slam thought the declarer, winning the opening lead. He played the ace of spades. One of the opponents showed out.

"No spades?" asked South. "No slam for you," replied the other defender.

What should the declarer have done?

Ask yourself what can go wrong. Sure, you can make seven spades if trumps are friendly, but you are in six spades. A 4/0 trump split is the danger and you can handle this problem by doing what?

Give up the overtrick and lead a low spade at Trick 2. If West has four, leading to the jack is fine. If East has four, you can negate it the same way.

On this hand, East has ♠Q1092, so after the jack loses to the queen, you can pick up the rest by going to dummy twice for repeated finesses.

DEAL 29   CAREFULL

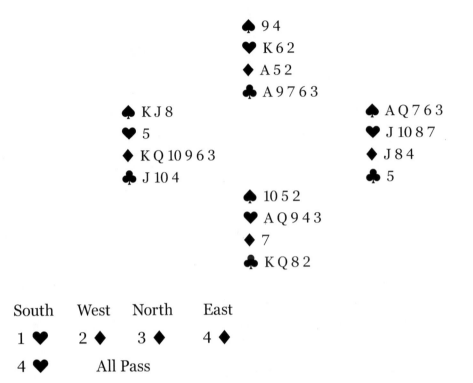

```
                    ♠ 9 4
                    ♥ K 6 2
                    ♦ A 5 2
                    ♣ A 9 7 6 3
   ♠ K J 8                          ♠ A Q 7 6 3
   ♥ 5                              ♥ J 10 8 7
   ♦ K Q 10 9 6 3                   ♦ J 8 4
   ♣ J 10 4                         ♣ 5
                    ♠ 10 5 2
                    ♥ A Q 9 4 3
                    ♦ 7
                    ♣ K Q 8 2
```

South	West	North	East
1 ♥	2 ♦	3 ♦	4 ♦
4 ♥	All Pass		

Opening Lead: ♦ King

Declarer won the opening lead and cashed the A-K of trumps. When West showed out on the second round of trumps, declarer couldn't cash the queen of trumps and start the clubs. East would ruff and cash the spades.

So declarer led a spade. East won and led the jack of hearts. Twist and turn, declarer had to lose four tricks. When comparing with his teammates, he found the other declarer had made an overtrick.

What did the other declarer do to make five hearts?

To guard against a 4/1 split, the only problem in this hand, the other declarer won the diamond ace at Trick 1. She then played a heart to the king, then a heart to her nine, not caring if it lost. At worst, she would lose one heart and two spade tricks.

When it won, she made an overtrick.

DEAL 30   DUMMY PROTECTION

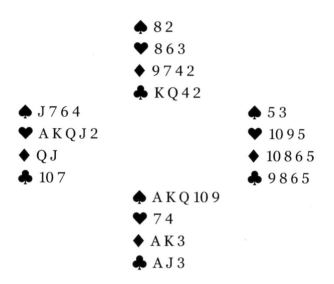

```
              ♠ 8 2
              ♥ 8 6 3
              ♦ 9 7 4 2
              ♣ K Q 4 2
♠ J 7 6 4                    ♠ 5 3
♥ A K Q J 2                  ♥ 10 9 5
♦ Q J                       ♦ 10 8 6 5
♣ 10 7                      ♣ 9 8 6 5
              ♠ A K Q 10 9
              ♥ 7 4
              ♦ A K 3
              ♣ A J 3
```

South	West	North	East
1 ♠	2 ♥	P	P
Dbl	P	2 ♠	P
3 ♠	P	4 ♠	All Pass

Opening Lead: ♥ Ace

Declarer ruffed the third round of hearts. He cashed the A-K-Q of spades. If he conceded a trump to West, he would lose two more hearts.

So he started the clubs. West ruffed the third round and led another heart. Declarer lost a diamond at the end. Down one.

How would you have solved the problem?

Declarer can afford to lose one trump trick, but he has to lose it early while there is a trump in dummy to handle the heart return. At Trick 4, instead of the top trumps, lead the ten.

West has to take it, but if he returns a heart, there is a trump in dummy. Declarer has the rest.

37

DEAL 31 GRAND THOUGHTS, BUT

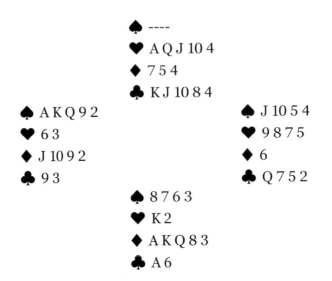

♠ ----
♥ A Q J 10 4
♦ 7 5 4
♣ K J 10 8 4

♠ A K Q 9 2
♥ 6 3
♦ J 10 9 2
♣ 9 3

♠ J 10 5 4
♥ 9 8 7 5
♦ 6
♣ Q 7 5 2

♠ 8 7 6 3
♥ K 2
♦ A K Q 8 3
♣ A 6

North	East	South	West
1 ♥	P	2 ♦	2 ♠
3 ♦	4 ♠	Dbl	P
5 ♦	P	6 ♦	All Pass

Opening Lead: ♠ Ace

Declarer was pleased with the dummy, seeing plenty of tricks. He ruffed the opening lead. "Might belong in seven hearts partner," said South.

"Please," thought North. "Just try to make six diamonds."

South cashed the A-K of trumps and thirteen tricks turned into eleven.

How would you have played six diamonds?

Declarer played as if he was in seven diamonds. But in six, to guard against a 4/1 trump division, declarer must duck the first round of trumps, leaving one in the dummy to take care of the spade return.

Then declarer has the rest of the tricks.

DEAL 32   CONTROL ISSUES

♠ K Q 8
♥ 9 7 5 4
♦ J 9 8 7
♣ 9 2

♠ 4
♥ Q 10 8 6 3
♦ A Q 6 5 3
♣ J 5

♠ J 10 6 5
♥ A J 2
♦ K 4 2
♣ Q 10 4

♠ A 9 7 3 2
♥ K
♦ 10
♣ A K 8 7 6 3

South	West	North	East
1♠	2♠*	P	3♥
P	P	3♠	All Pass

* Michaels; Hearts and a minor

Contract: 3 ♠
Opening Lead: ♥ 6

East won the opening lead and continued the suit. Declarer ruffed, cashed the A-K of clubs and played a third club. When West discarded, South ruffed with dummy's eight.

Declarer cashed the K-Q of spades, West showing out on the second round. South crossed back to his hand by ruffing leaving himself with one trump. Since East had two high trumps, South had no more tricks. Down one.

How could South have avoided shortening himself?

At the other table, play started the same. But when declarer played the K-Q of spades, he overtook with the ace to reach his hand. If trumps were 3/2, he would lose one trump trick and make four spades.

If trumps were 4/1, he could continue playing clubs, letting a defender ruff in, but keep control of the hand. Making three spades.

DEAL 33   A RIGHT TIME AND A WRONG TIME

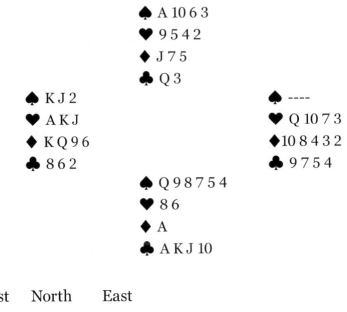

```
                    ♠ A 10 6 3
                    ♥ 9 5 4 2
                    ♦ J 7 5
                    ♣ Q 3
      ♠ K J 2                        ♠ ----
      ♥ A K J                        ♥ Q 10 7 3
      ♦ K Q 9 6                      ♦ 10 8 4 3 2
      ♣ 8 6 2                        ♣ 9 7 5 4
                    ♠ Q 9 8 7 5 4
                    ♥ 8 6
                    ♦ A
                    ♣ A K J 10
```

South	West	North	East
1 ♠	1 NT	2 ♠	P
3 ♠	P	4 ♠	All Pass

Opening Lead: ♥ Ace

West led the heart ace and continued with the king and jack. Declarer ruffed the third round. Declarer now could afford to lose one trump trick. The normal safety play here is low to the ten; if both follow, declarer only loses one trick.

But if East wins the jack and plays a heart, West will overruff declarer. So declarer played a low spade to the ace and went down one when East showed out.

How would you have solved declarer's dilemma?

The other declarer used the additional information available. West was known to have the spade king. So she led the queen of spades; West had to cover and the problem was solved.

DEAL 34   NO PROBLEM

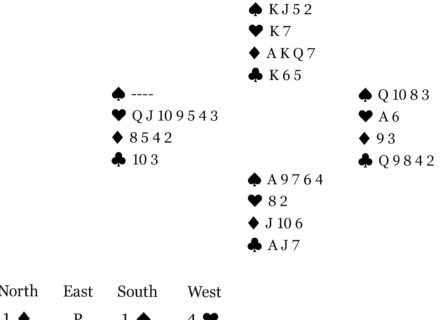

♠ K J 5 2
♥ K 7
♦ A K Q 7
♣ K 6 5

♠ ----
♥ Q J 10 9 5 4 3
♦ 8 5 4 2
♣ 10 3

♠ Q 10 8 3
♥ A 6
♦ 9 3
♣ Q 9 8 4 2

♠ A 9 7 6 4
♥ 8 2
♦ J 10 6
♣ A J 7

North	East	South	West
1 ♦	P	1 ♠	4 ♥
4 ♠		All Pass	

Opening Lead: ♥ Queen

The defense took the first two heart tricks. East returned a diamond. If the spades divide 2/2, declarer has the rest. If 3/1, there is a likely trump loser which declarer can afford. But what about 4/0?

Is there a line of play to guard against 4/0 in either hand?

While on this auction, East is more likely to have spade length, declarer has a perfect safety play against either defender.

He starts low to the king. When West shows out, he leads from dummy. East plays the ten, South wins and East is held to one trick.

If East had shown out, now a spade to the ace and low towards the jack would limit West to one trick.

41

DEAL 35   ANYTHING BUT

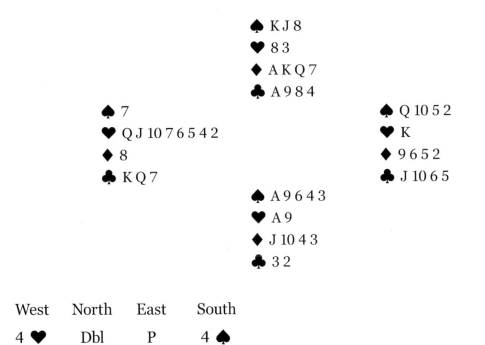

♠ K J 8
♥ 8 3
♦ A K Q 7
♣ A 9 8 4

♠ 7
♥ Q J 10 7 6 5 4 2
♦ 8
♣ K Q 7

♠ Q 10 5 2
♥ K
♦ 9 6 5 2
♣ J 10 6 5

♠ A 9 6 4 3
♥ A 9
♦ J 10 4 3
♣ 3 2

West	North	East	South
4 ♥	Dbl	P	4 ♠
All Pass			

Opening Lead: ♥ Queen

Declarer won the opening lead and with a heart and a club loser, he wanted to hold his trump losers to one. He cashed the ace of spades, then led low towards the dummy. Not a very good plan. Down one.

How did the declarer at the other table make four spades?

The only danger is one defender holding four trumps to the ♠Q10xx. The usual play holding ♠A5432 opposite ♠KJ6 is to play the ace, then finesse the jack. But having the nine gives you more options.

On this hand the only player who might have four spades is East. So one good play is lead to the jack. If that play loses to the queen, you can cash the king.
When West shows out, you will finesse East out of his ten. Another option is to start low to the king, then back to the nine.
Anything but the ace first.

DEAL 36   DANGER HAND CONSIDERATIONS

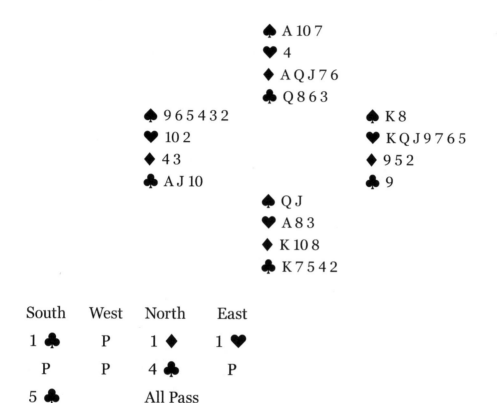

```
                    ♠ A 10 7
                    ♥ 4
                    ♦ A Q J 7 6
                    ♣ Q 8 6 3
        ♠ 9 6 5 4 3 2                    ♠ K 8
        ♥ 10 2                           ♥ K Q J 9 7 6 5
        ♦ 4 3                            ♦ 9 5 2
        ♣ A J 10                         ♣ 9
                    ♠ Q J
                    ♥ A 8 3
                    ♦ K 10 8
                    ♣ K 7 5 4 2
```

South	West	North	East
1 ♣	P	1 ♦	1 ♥
P	P	4 ♣	P
5 ♣		All Pass	

Opening Lead: ♥ 10

With one sure club and probably one spade loser, declarer was concerned about not losing two trump tricks. From the bidding, South guessed that East was more likely to hold the club ace, so he went to dummy to lead a club to his king.

West won the ace and switched to a spade. Now the spade king rated to be with East and it was all downhill, West having started with the ♣AJ10.

Why was it better to play the trumps the other way around?

Declarer can afford to lose two trump tricks, just not a spade trick, too. If the club queen loses to the ace, East can't attack spades. Declarer can win any return, play the club king and just keep playing diamonds.

If there is still an outstanding trump, the opponents are welcome to it anytime.

DEAL 37   WHAT CAN GO WRONG?

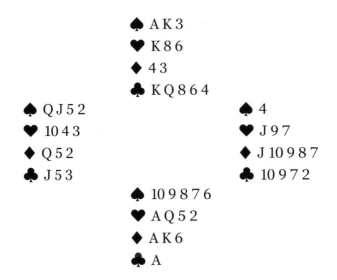

♠ A K 3
♥ K 8 6
♦ 4 3
♣ K Q 8 6 4

♠ Q J 5 2   ♠ 4
♥ 10 4 3   ♥ J 9 7
♦ Q 5 2   ♦ J 10 9 8 7
♣ J 5 3   ♣ 10 9 7 2

♠ 10 9 8 7 6
♥ A Q 5 2
♦ A K 6
♣ A

Contract: 6 ♠

Opening Lead: ♦ 2

Declarer won the opening lead. He played a low spade to the ace, both opponents followed. When he cashed the king, East showed out.

Down one.

What do you think North is saying to South?

At the other table, declarer asked herself "What can go wrong?".

Well, if East has ♠QJxx, I can't help it. But what about West?

So she first played a low spade to the ace, everyone followed. She crossed back to her hand and led the spade ten. When West followed low, she played low from dummy, not caring if it won or lost and the contract was assured.

DEAL 38   NOT AGAIN?

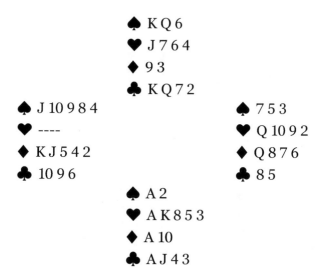

♠ K Q 6
♥ J 7 6 4
♦ 9 3
♣ K Q 7 2

♠ J 10 9 8 4
♥ ----
♦ K J 5 4 2
♣ 10 9 6

♠ 7 5 3
♥ Q 10 9 2
♦ Q 8 7 6
♣ 8 5

♠ A 2
♥ A K 8 5 3
♦ A 10
♣ A J 4 3

Contract: 6 ♥

Opening Lead: ♠ Jack

Declarer won the opening lead in hand. He played the heart ace, one opponent showed out. There was no recovery.

How did the declarer at the other table make six hearts?

By asking what can go wrong? The only jeopardy to six hearts is a 4/0 trump split. She took a safety play by leading a low heart at Trick 2.

If West had four hearts, he could take the queen and the contract was safe.

If East had four, he too could take the queen, but declarer could pick up the remaining ♥1092.

KEEPING

CONTROL

DEAL 39   KEEPING CONTROL

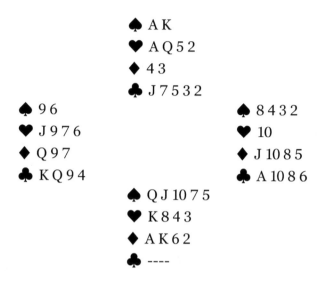

```
                    ♠ A K
                    ♥ A Q 5 2
                    ♦ 4 3
                    ♣ J 7 5 3 2
    ♠ 9 6                         ♠ 8 4 3 2
    ♥ J 9 7 6                     ♥ 10
    ♦ Q 9 7                       ♦ J 10 8 5
    ♣ K Q 9 4                     ♣ A 10 8 6
                    ♠ Q J 10 7 5
                    ♥ K 8 4 3
                    ♦ A K 6 2
                    ♣ ----
```

Contract: 6 ♥
Opening Lead: ♣ King

South ruffed the opening lead and cashed the A-K of trumps. With a 3/2 break, he could ruff another club, lead a spade to dummy, draw the missing trumps and take five spades, four trumps, two diamonds and two club ruffs, thirteen tricks.

But when East discarded on the second high trump, declarer was doomed. He ruffed a club, cashed the A-K of spades and crossed to the ace of diamonds.

He led a high spade hoping to discard clubs. West ruffed and the defense won two club tricks. Down two.

How would you handle this bad trump break to make six hearts?

The contract is six hearts, not seven. You need to lose a trump trick while you can still take a club ruff in hand. At Trick 2, play a small trump from both hands.

When both opponents follow, twelve tricks are assured.

DEAL 40   CONTROLLING A 4/0 TRUMP SPLIT

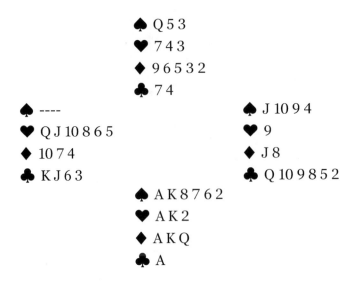

```
                    ♠ Q 5 3
                    ♥ 7 4 3
                    ♦ 9 6 5 3 2
                    ♣ 7 4
        ♠ ----                      ♠ J 10 9 4
        ♥ Q J 10 8 6 5              ♥ 9
        ♦ 10 7 4                    ♦ J 8
        ♣ K J 6 3                   ♣ Q 10 9 8 5 2
                    ♠ A K 8 7 6 2
                    ♥ A K 2
                    ♦ A K Q
                    ♣ A
```

Contract: 6 ♠

Opening Lead: ♥ Queen

In a team game, declarer, not thinking what could go wrong, won the opening lead and made the "natural" looking play of a low spade to the queen. There was no recovery, losing a spade and a heart.

Could you have handled the 4/0 trump split?

At the other table, the declarer did ask herself what could go wrong and played trumps with the ace first. OK, bad news. But declarer can recover. She cashed the three high diamonds.

If diamonds are 3/2, everything is all right. If East has three, you can cross to the spade queen and lead a diamond, discarding your losing heart, not caring if East ruffs.

If East started with two diamonds and ruffs your third high diamond, declarer wins the return and draws trumps ending in the dummy to discard the heart loser. If East does not ruff, declarer crosses to dummy and plays another diamond. Twelve tricks either way.

DEAL 41   STAYING OUT OF TROUBLE

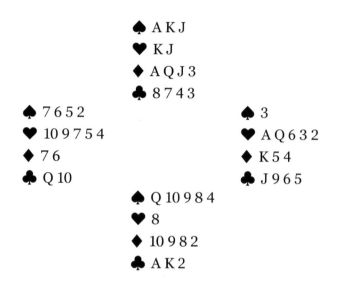

```
                        ♠ A K J
                        ♥ K J
                        ♦ A Q J 3
                        ♣ 8 7 4 3
        ♠ 7 6 5 2                        ♠ 3
        ♥ 10 9 7 5 4                     ♥ A Q 6 3 2
        ♦ 7 6                            ♦ K 5 4
        ♣ Q 10                           ♣ J 9 6 5
                        ♠ Q 10 9 8 4
                        ♥ 8
                        ♦ 10 9 8 2
                        ♣ A K 2
```

North	East	South	West
1 ♦	1 ♥	1 ♠	3 ♥
3 ♠	P	4 ♠	All Pass

Opening Lead: ♥ 10

East won the heart queen and continued the heart ace. Declarer looking at the quality, not the quantity of his trump holding, ruffed. He played the A-K of spades, East showed out on the second spade.

Declarer came to the ace of clubs and took a losing diamond finesse. East played back another club. Declarer was in trouble.

How did the other declarer maintain trump control?

At Trick 2, instead of ruffing, she discarded the two of clubs, a trick she would lose anyhow. East switched to a club.

Declarer drew trumps, lost a diamond finesse and now could take the rest.

49

DEAL 42   STAYING ONE STEP AHEAD

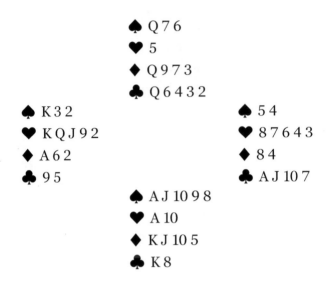

```
                    ♠ Q 7 6
                    ♥ 5
                    ♦ Q 9 7 3
                    ♣ Q 6 4 3 2
    ♠ K 3 2                        ♠ 5 4
    ♥ K Q J 9 2                    ♥ 8 7 6 4 3
    ♦ A 6 2                        ♦ 8 4
    ♣ 9 5                          ♣ A J 10 7
                    ♠ A J 10 9 8
                    ♥ A 10
                    ♦ K J 10 5
                    ♣ K 8
```

South	West	North	East
1 ♠	2 ♥	2 ♠	3 ♥
4 ♠		All Pass	

Opening Lead: ♥ King

Declarer won the opening lead and ruffed his remaining heart. He led the spade queen and finessed. When West ducked, declarer repeated the finesse. West won and played another heart.

Declarer lost control of the hand before he could set up his ten winners.

How would you have kept control?

You want to stay one step ahead of the defenders forcing you in hearts. So win the second round of trumps and go about your business of the missing aces.

Or an alternative plan is to go after those aces after ruffing the heart. There is still a trump in dummy to handle the heart return.

DEAL 43   QUANTITY OVER QUALITY

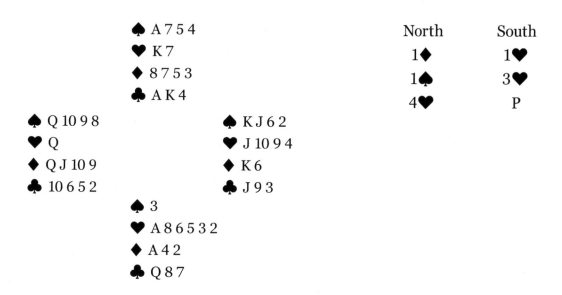

	North	South
	1♦	1♥
	1♠	3♥
	4♥	P

Contract: 4 ♥

Opening Lead: ♦ Queen

What can go wrong? The usual question. Declarer won the opening lead and played A-K of trumps. And he was in trouble. He ended losing two diamonds and two trumps, down one. He didn't ask himself that question.

Unlucky, or with proper planning could you have made four hearts?

If trumps are 3/2, the bellman is making the hand. So win the diamond, play a spade to the ace and ruff a spade. Cash the heart ace and a heart to the king. Sure enough, 4/1. So the bellman is going down at the other table. Ruff another spade.

You only have two trumps left. So does East and his are bigger. Play three rounds of clubs, ending in dummy. Hey, you are entitled to a little good luck, too.

Now you have nine tricks in the bank. Lead your last spade. East can't stop you from winning one more trump trick.

Your trumps were not very good, but you had a lot of them. Quantity beat quality.

DEAL 44   MAKE AN OFFER

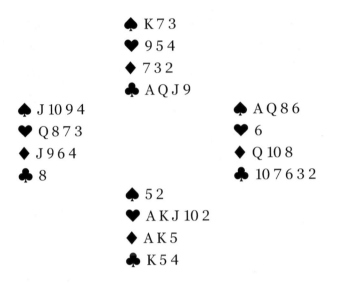

♠ K 7 3
♥ 9 5 4
♦ 7 3 2
♣ A Q J 9

♠ J 10 9 4
♥ Q 8 7 3
♦ J 9 6 4
♣ 8

♠ A Q 8 6
♥ 6
♦ Q 10 8
♣ 10 7 6 3 2

♠ 5 2
♥ A K J 10 2
♦ A K 5
♣ K 5 4

Contract: 4 ♥
Opening Lead: ♠ Jack

Declarer ruffed the third spade (not best) and cashed the heart ace. He crossed to dummy with a club and led a heart. When East showed out, declarer played the jack but West ducked.

Declarer cashed the heart king and started the clubs. West ruffed the third club and led another spade. South still had a diamond loser. Down one.

What's the best line of play to handle the 4/1 trump split?

In order to keep control, lose your trump trick early. At Trick 4, lead the ♥J. If West ducks, make him another offer. Lead the ♥10. West is helpless.

If he wins and leads another spade, there is still a trump in dummy. Declarer draws the rest of the trumps and runs the clubs. Ten tricks.

DEAL 45   WHAT'S THE SAFEST WAY?

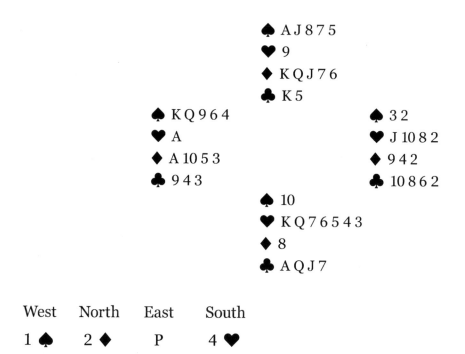

```
              ♠ A J 8 7 5
              ♥ 9
              ♦ K Q J 7 6
              ♣ K 5
♠ K Q 9 6 4                    ♠ 3 2
♥ A                            ♥ J 10 8 2
♦ A 10 5 3                     ♦ 9 4 2
♣ 9 4 3                        ♣ 10 8 6 2
              ♠ 10
              ♥ K Q 7 6 5 4 3
              ♦ 8
              ♣ A Q J 7
```

West	North	East	South
1 ♠	2 ♦	P	4 ♥
All Pass			

Opening Lead: ♠ King

Declarer saw that she had two quick losers, the two missing aces. If she could hold her trump losers to two, the contract was safe. If trumps are 3/2, easy.

If West has ♥AJ108, there is nothing declarer can do. Declarer led a trump to the king, losing to the ace. When East held ♥J1082, she lost two more trump tricks, down one.

Was this foreseeable or unlucky?

There are only 14 HCP's missing. Who has the ace of trumps? The janitor knows West has it.

So to cater to a 4/1 split with West's ace being singleton, the first trump play should be low from both hands.

53

DEAL 46   FINESSE EVERYBODY

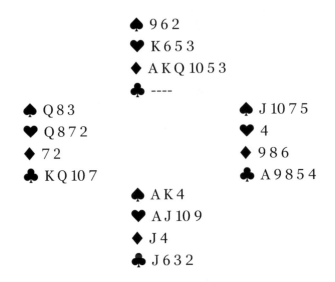

♠ 9 6 2
♥ K 6 5 3
♦ A K Q 10 5 3
♣ ----

♠ Q 8 3
♥ Q 8 7 2
♦ 7 2
♣ K Q 10 7

♠ J 10 7 5
♥ 4
♦ 9 8 6
♣ A 9 8 5 4

♠ A K 4
♥ A J 10 9
♦ J 4
♣ J 6 3 2

Contract: 6 ♥

Opening Lead: ♣ King

Declarer envisioned eight tricks in spades and diamonds, just a matter of clearing the trumps. He ruffed the opening lead and led a small heart to the jack, winning. Had it lost, he planned to win the return, draw trumps and claim. So he crossed back to dummy's king of hearts and repeated the finesse. Oops!

Control of the trumps had now passed to West. Declarer was unable to make use of dummy's diamonds, West being able to ruff in, and declarer had far too many losers.

Was there a way to counter West's quick-witted defense?

Sure. After a "successful" finesse against East, take a finesse against West for the same card. Play the heart ten and let it ride if West plays low. You must get the queen of trumps out in order to maintain control.

Even if East scores an unnecessary trick, you have the rest. The king of hearts in dummy takes care of a club return.

DEAL 47   GET OUT OF THE WAY

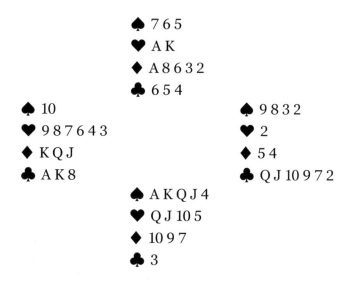

♠ 7 6 5
♥ A K
♦ A 8 6 3 2
♣ 6 5 4

♠ 10
♥ 9 8 7 6 4 3
♦ K Q J
♣ A K 8

♠ 9 8 3 2
♥ 2
♦ 5 4
♣ Q J 10 9 7 2

♠ A K Q J 4
♥ Q J 10 5
♦ 10 9 7
♣ 3

South	West	North	East
1 ♠	2 ♥	Dbl	P
2 ♠	P	4 ♠	All Pass

Opening Lead: ♣ Ace

West led the club ace, East encouraged, and West continued another club. Declarer ruffed. Declarer played the A-K of trumps, West followed once, then discarded a heart.

Declarer played the A-K of hearts, trying to get out of his own way, but East ruffed the second heart, not a big surprise. South still had two diamond losers. Down one.

How did the other declarer make four spades?

At the other table, play started the same way. But declarer only cashed one round of hearts. Then she continued spades, discarding dummy's remaining king of hearts under the spades. After drawing trumps, she cashed the Q-J-10 of hearts.

She had ten tricks.

DEAL 48   AVOIDING BEING TAPPED OUT

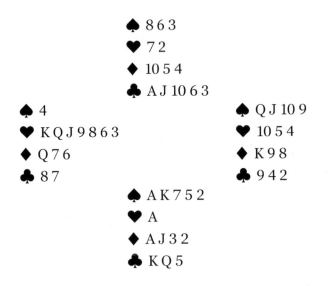

```
                    ♠ 8 6 3
                    ♥ 7 2
                    ♦ 10 5 4
                    ♣ A J 10 6 3
    ♠ 4                          ♠ Q J 10 9
    ♥ K Q J 9 8 6 3              ♥ 10 5 4
    ♦ Q 7 6                      ♦ K 9 8
    ♣ 8 7                        ♣ 9 4 2
                    ♠ A K 7 5 2
                    ♥ A
                    ♦ A J 3 2
                    ♣ K Q 5
```

South	West	North	East
1 ♠	3 ♥	P	P
Dbl	P	3 ♠	P
4 ♠	All Pass		

Opening Lead: ♥ King

South won the opening lead and cashed the A-K of trumps. When West discarded, South led a third trump. East won and led another heart. South ruffed but he couldn't afford to lead a fourth trump, so he started the clubs.

East ruffed the fourth club and led his last heart. South still had to lose two diamonds. Down one.

Given the bidding, was there a better line of play?

South ignored the danger of a 4-1 trump split, not unlikely given the bidding. At Trick 2 South should lead a low trump. East wins and returns a heart. South can ruff and lead another low trump.

East can't gain this time with a heart return because now South can ruff in dummy. If East shifts to a diamond, South wins, draws trumps and runs the clubs for ten tricks.

DEAL 49   GREEDY

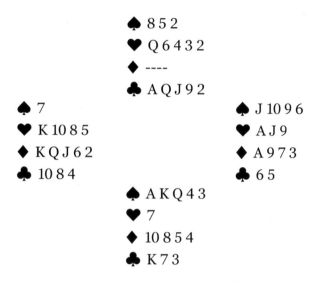

♠ 8 5 2
♥ Q 6 4 3 2
♦ ----
♣ A Q J 9 2

♠ 7
♥ K 10 8 5
♦ K Q J 6 2
♣ 10 8 4

♠ J 10 9 6
♥ A J 9
♦ A 9 7 3
♣ 6 5

♠ A K Q 4 3
♥ 7
♦ 10 8 5 4
♣ K 7 3

Contract: 4 ♠
Opening Lead: ♦ King

South ruffed the opening lead and counted 11 or 12 tricks; 5 spades in hand, some diamond ruffs, and 5 clubs. At Trick 2, South played a club to his king, ruffed a second diamond and cashed the A-K of trumps.

When West showed out, South cashed the spade queen and tried running the clubs. East ruffed the third club and the defense took two diamonds and one heart for down one. So much for 11 or 12 tricks.

How should declarer play to make ten tricks?

Since the contract was four spades, declarer should allow for a possible 4-1 trump split. He can lead a spade from dummy at Trick 2 and play low from his hand.

If West wins and returns a trump, declarer can draw the remaining trumps and run the clubs. He scores five clubs, four trumps in hand and one diamond ruff. Ten tricks.

DEAL 50   HARRY S

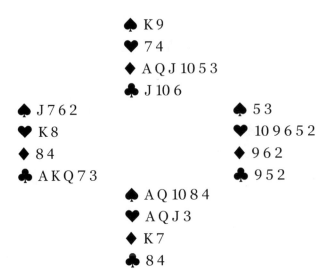

♠ K 9
♥ 7 4
♦ A Q J 10 5 3
♣ J 10 6

♠ J 7 6 2
♥ K 8
♦ 8 4
♣ A K Q 7 3

♠ 5 3
♥ 10 9 6 5 2
♦ 9 6 2
♣ 9 5 2

♠ A Q 10 8 4
♥ A Q J 3
♦ K 7
♣ 8 4

South	West	North	East
1 ♠	2 ♣	2 ♦	P
2 ♥	P	3 ♦	P
4 ♦	P	4 ♠	All Pass

Opening Lead: ♣ Ace

West led the top three clubs, South ruffing the third. He played a spade to the king, then a spade to the ace and queen. Oh, oh. He had no winning options.

If he conceded a trump, West would cash two clubs. If he tried to run the diamonds, West would ruff in and he had no way back to the diamonds.

Down one. Sad.

How did another declarer make four spades?

Another declarer realized that if trumps were 3/2, he had the rest of the tricks. But if they were 4/1? At Trick 4 declarer played a spade to the nine, not caring if it lost to the jack. He could win the return, draw trumps and run the diamonds.

And if the nine wins? West will look suspiciously at South and hold his cards closer to his chest. "Who are you," he might ask, "Harry Stappenbeck?"

Note: The late Harry Stappenbeck, 6 ft, 11 inches, was the world's tallest bridge expert. It was virtually impossible for him not to see into your hand.

DEAL 51   HARRY'S COUSIN

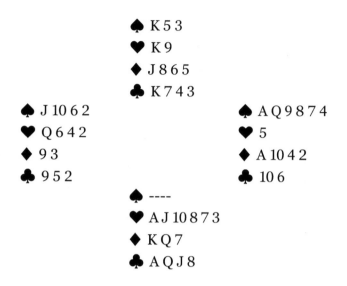

♠ K 5 3
♥ K 9
♦ J 8 6 5
♣ K 7 4 3

♠ J 10 6 2
♥ Q 6 4 2
♦ 9 3
♣ 9 5 2

♠ A Q 9 8 7 4
♥ 5
♦ A 10 4 2
♣ 10 6

♠ ----
♥ A J 10 8 7 3
♦ K Q 7
♣ A Q J 8

South	West	North	East
1 ♥	P	1 NT	2 ♠
3 ♣	3 ♠	3 NT	4 ♠
5 ♥		All Pass	

Opening Lead: ♠ Jack

Declarer ruffed the opening lead. She played a trump to the king and returned a trump, playing the jack as East discarded. West led another spade, South ruffing. South drew the rest of the trumps, leaving her with none.

After cashing four clubs, she lost the rest. Down two.

Could you have kept better control and survived the five level?

At the other table, at Trick 2 declarer led a trump to dummy's nine. If it lost to the queen, East was the safe hand. He couldn't continue spades. Declarer lost only two tricks.

"That's twice you played a trump to the nine," said West. "Are you sure you aren't related to Harry?"

DEAL 52   SNEAKY

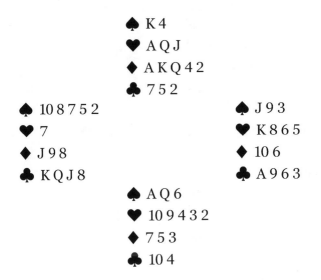

♠ K 4
♥ A Q J
♦ A K Q 4 2
♣ 7 5 2

♠ 10 8 7 5 2
♥ 7
♦ J 9 8
♣ K Q J 8

♠ J 9 3
♥ K 8 6 5
♦ 10 6
♣ A 9 6 3

♠ A Q 6
♥ 10 9 4 3 2
♦ 7 5 3
♣ 10 4

Contract: 4 ♥

Opening Lead: ♣ King

The defense started with three rounds of clubs. Declarer ruffed the third round. and played a trump to the queen, winning. He played a spade to his hand to repeat the finesse. When West showed out, declarer was doomed.

If South played ace, then the jack, East would win and continue clubs, creating another trump trick for herself. If he played the jack, a spade return would block the spades. Declarer would be unable to draw the last trump.

How did the other declarer make four hearts?

Declarer can afford to lose two clubs and a heart, he just can't lose control. After the first trump finesse wins, lead the heart jack. Give them their trick while there is still a trump in dummy to handle a club return.

With a spade return, you can win the king and cash the trump ace. Now you can come back to your hand with a spade to draw the last trump.

Don't trust those sneaky opponents.

DEAL 53   SHORTNESS? BEWARE

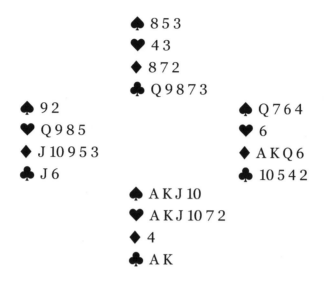

```
                    ♠ 8 5 3
                    ♥ 4 3
                    ♦ 8 7 2
                    ♣ Q 9 8 7 3
        ♠ 9 2                      ♠ Q 7 6 4
        ♥ Q 9 8 5                  ♥ 6
        ♦ J 10 9 5 3               ♦ A K Q 6
        ♣ J 6                      ♣ 10 5 4 2
                    ♠ A K J 10
                    ♥ A K J 10 7 2
                    ♦ 4
                    ♣ A K
```

Contract: 4 ♥

Opening Lead: ♦ Jack

Declarer ruffed the second diamond. He cashed the A-K of trumps and saw East show out. Such a nice hand, but the handwriting was on the wall. He continued with the trump jack. West won and led another diamond.

The declarer could only draw trumps and hope. But being out of trumps, he still had to lose a spade and another diamond.

Could you have managed to bring this beauty home?

Remember the general principle, lose them early. To avoid being tapped out, try to keep a trump in dummy. Declarer can afford to lose one spade, one heart, and one diamond. What declarer cannot afford to lose is control. Anytime you have shortness, beware.

Another declarer ruffed the second diamond, but he started the trumps by playing the trump jack. West won and led another diamond. Declarer ruffed and now gave up another loser, the spade jack.

Since there was still a trump in dummy, another diamond force was useless. East returned a club. Declarer won, drew trumps and claimed.

DEAL 54   WHICH ONE WILL DO?

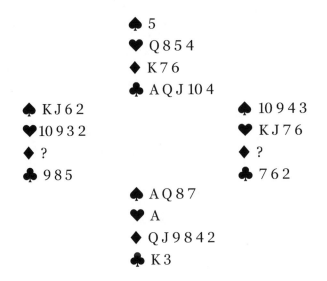

```
                    ♠ 5
                    ♥ Q 8 5 4
                    ♦ K 7 6
                    ♣ A Q J 10 4
        ♠ K J 6 2                    ♠ 10 9 4 3
        ♥ 10 9 3 2                   ♥ K J 7 6
        ♦ ?                          ♦ ?
        ♣ 9 8 5                      ♣ 7 6 2
                    ♠ A Q 8 7
                    ♥ A
                    ♦ Q J 9 8 4 2
                    ♣ K 3
```

Contract: 6 ♦

Opening Lead: ♥ Jack

Declarer made the natural looking play in the trump suit of low to the king. Was she successful? If trumps divide 2/2 or 3/1 there is no problem.

If one opponent has all four diamonds, about a 10% chance you want to cater to that. Half of the time it will be East, half the time West.

How did the above declarer do?

If East has ♦A1053 she was OK. But what if it was West? To cater to either, declarer should first lead the one card that would cater to either, the queen of diamonds.

Note: The above East/West cards obviously will change depending on which hand has four diamonds.

DEAL 55   AN EARLY INSTINCTIVE PLAY

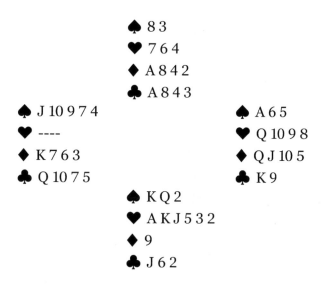

♠ 8 3
♥ 7 6 4
♦ A 8 4 2
♣ A 8 4 3

♠ J 10 9 7 4
♥ ----
♦ K 7 6 3
♣ Q 10 7 5

♠ A 6 5
♥ Q 10 9 8
♦ Q J 10 5
♣ K 9

♠ K Q 2
♥ A K J 5 3 2
♦ 9
♣ J 6 2

Contract: 4 ♥

Opening Lead: ♠ Jack

East won the opening lead and returned the diamond queen. Declarer was facing two club losers, barring a miracle. With nine trumps, he played a heart to the ace. West showed out. He lost one spade, two clubs and a heart. Down one

Can you make four hearts. How?

Another declarer, a little more experienced, made the expert play of ruffing a diamond at Trick 3. After cashing the trump ace, he realized he might win the race, winning ten tricks before they could win four.

He cashed the spade king and ruffed the good spade queen to get an extra entry. A diamond ruff was followed by a club to the ace and another diamond ruff. Having won eight tricks, this was the position with four tricks to be played:

North: ♠ ----   ♥ 7   ♦ ----   ♣ 8 4 3   East

                                                            ♠ ----   ♥ Q 10 9   ♦ ----   ♣ K

South: ♠ ----   ♥ K J   ♦ ----   ♣ J 6

South exited a club and waited for two trump tricks. The key play was the early diamond ruff. It would not have mattered which defender had all the trumps.

DEAL 56   STAY IN THE PRESENT MOMENT

♠ A 5 4 3
♥ A K Q
♦ 10 7 2
♣ A J 10

♠ K Q 9 7 2
♥ ----
♦ 9 6 3
♣ K Q 9 8 7

Contract: 4 ♠
Opening Lead: ♦ King

As North tabled the dummy, declarer said, "You have the wrong red cards, partner." If North could have switched his hearts and diamonds, seven spades was possible.

After the opponents cashed three diamond tricks and switched to a heart, declarer, still thinking about "the grand," played a spade to his king.

When West showed out, he was down in game.

What should declarer have been thinking about?

Think about what you are in, not what "could" have been. Think about what can go wrong. The only problem at hand now was the trump suit. If spades were 2/2 or 3/1, game was cold. But what about 4/0?

If West has four you can't do anything about it. But if East has four, you will find out by starting with the spade ace and be able to handle the 4/0 break.

East's spades: ♠ J 10 8 6
West's spades: ♠ void

64

DEAL 57   WHICH SIDE?

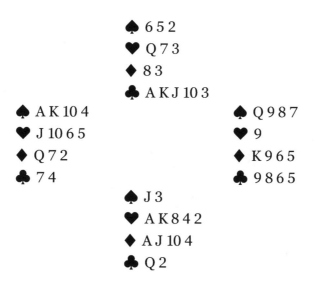

♠ 6 5 2
♥ Q 7 3
♦ 8 3
♣ A K J 10 3

♠ A K 10 4
♥ J 10 6 5
♦ Q 7 2
♣ 7 4

♠ Q 9 8 7
♥ 9
♦ K 9 6 5
♣ 9 8 6 5

♠ J 3
♥ A K 8 4 2
♦ A J 10 4
♣ Q 2

Contract: 4 ♥

Opening Lead: ♠ Ace

In a team game, the defense began with three rounds of spades, South ruffing the third round. It's an easy game. Draw trumps, cash the clubs, eleven tricks.

Declarer tried to draw three rounds of trumps, playing low to the queen, the short side first, but now he was stuck.

He couldn't run the clubs. West would ruff in and win a diamond trick later.

What's the best play? A 4/1 split occurs often enough to consider this.

At the other table, declarer played the A-K of trumps first. If they split, she could go to the trump queen and claim. If 4/1, she can just keep those clubs coming.

West could ruff in anytime, but the trump queen was the entry to dummy.

DEAL 58   PREVENTING A HEADACHE

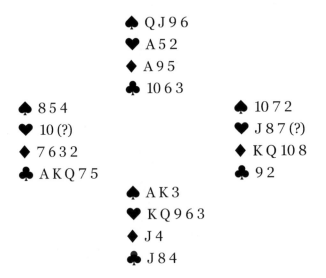

♠ Q J 9 6
♥ A 5 2
♦ A 9 5
♣ 10 6 3

♠ 8 5 4
♥ 10 (?)
♦ 7 6 3 2
♣ A K Q 7 5

♠ 10 7 2
♥ J 8 7 (?)
♦ K Q 10 8
♣ 9 2

♠ A K 3
♥ K Q 9 6 3
♦ J 4
♣ J 8 4

Contract: 4 ♥

Opening Lead: ♣ Ace

West leads the A-K-Q of clubs, then the seven of diamonds. Declarer needs the rest of the tricks. The diamond can go on the spade, but first he has to play the hearts. If they are 3/2, great.

Playing to the honor in the short side, he led towards dummy's ♥A, West playing the ♥10, East the ♥4. When he led a small heart from dummy, East played the ♥7. Finesse or not?

If trumps are 4/1, he needed a singleton 10 or jack. Was that ten a singleton or wasn't it?

He played the _____. Down one.

How could all this headache have been prevented?

Declarer is in trouble only if trumps are 4/1 and if so, will need a singleton ♥10 or ♥J. Play the ♥K first, then lead towards dummy. West shows out on the second round. Problem solved. Cancel the aspirin.

Making four hearts.

DEAL 59   KEEPING CONTROL

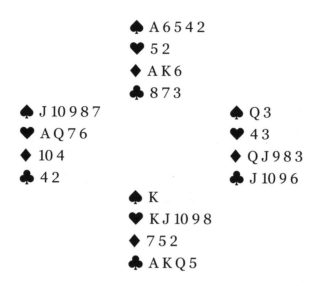

♠ A 6 5 4 2
♥ 5 2
♦ A K 6
♣ 8 7 3

♠ J 10 9 8 7
♥ A Q 7 6
♦ 10 4
♣ 4 2

♠ Q 3
♥ 4 3
♦ Q J 9 8 3
♣ J 10 9 6

♠ K
♥ K J 10 9 8
♦ 7 5 2
♣ A K Q 5

Contract: 4 ♥
Opening Lead: ♠ Jack

3NT would have probably been better, but here you are. Declarer won the spade in hand and played a diamond to dummy. He returned a heart, ducked all around. Declarer went back to the diamond king, discarded his last diamond on the spade ace. and led another heart.

This time West won the queen and played another spade, South ruffing. West won the next trump and forced South to ruff another spade with his last trump.

Declarer had lost control. He took two high clubs, but West scored the last two tricks with a trump and a spade.

Could South have prevailed after West's good defense?

To assure his contract, South should lead the king of trumps at Trick 2. He has time to force out both high honors, draw trumps, scoring three trumps, three clubs, two diamonds and two spades.

DEAL 60   MAKE AN OFFER

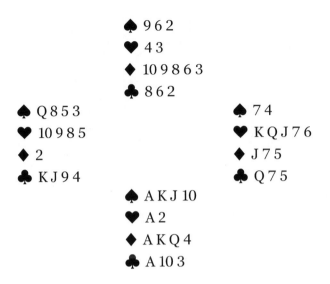

♠ 9 6 2
♥ 4 3
♦ 10 9 8 6 3
♣ 8 6 2

♠ Q 8 5 3
♥ 10 9 8 5
♦ 2
♣ K J 9 4

♠ 7 4
♥ K Q J 7 6
♦ J 7 5
♣ Q 7 5

♠ A K J 10
♥ A 2
♦ A K Q 4
♣ A 10 3

N/S Vul

South	West	North	East
2♣	P	2♦	2♥
2♠	3♥	P	P
3NT	P	4♠	All Pass

Opening Lead: ♥ 10

East/West made a lot of noise, putting South into an uncomfortable 4/3 spade contract. South hoped for the best (unlikely) and played A-K of spades and another spade. Very unsuccessful, still adding up the undertricks.

Can you make four spades?

After the same opening lead, lead spades, but not the ace, the TEN!

If the defense wins and leads a heart, dummy can ruff heart continuations.

And if the defense ducks the ten? Lead the JACK! This they can take but again declarer still has a trump in dummy.

As long as spades are no worse than 4/1, this contract is coming home.

DEAL 61   KEEPING CONTROL OF YOUR TRUMPS

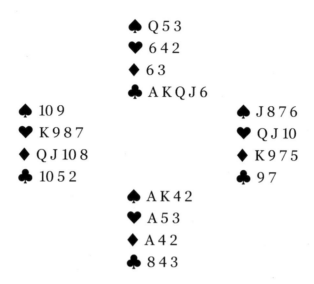

♠ Q 5 3
♥ 6 4 2
♦ 6 3
♣ A K Q J 6

♠ 10 9
♥ K 9 8 7
♦ Q J 10 8
♣ 10 5 2

♠ J 8 7 6
♥ Q J 10
♦ K 9 7 5
♣ 9 7

♠ A K 4 2
♥ A 5 3
♦ A 4 2
♣ 8 4 3

Contract: 4 ♠

Opening Lead: ♦ Queen

South won the opening lead and returned a diamond. East won and shifted to the heart queen. South won, ruffed his last diamond and cashed the three top trumps.

When West discarded, declarer tried to run the clubs. East ruffed the third club and cashed two hearts for down one.

Was there a better line of play? How can declarer keep better control?

If you have to lose a trump trick (likely), lose it early. Play a low trump from each hand at Trick 2. What can the defense do?

At best, the defense can cash a diamond. Declarer gets in, draws trumps and runs the clubs for ten tricks.

DEAL 62   DRAWING TRUMPS: KEEPING CONTROL

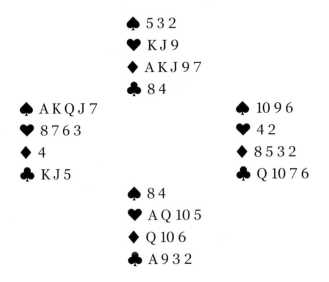

```
                    ♠ 5 3 2
                    ♥ K J 9
                    ♦ A K J 9 7
                    ♣ 8 4
    ♠ A K Q J 7                    ♠ 10 9 6
    ♥ 8 7 6 3                      ♥ 4 2
    ♦ 4                            ♦ 8 5 3 2
    ♣ K J 5                        ♣ Q 10 7 6
                    ♠ 8 4
                    ♥ A Q 10 5
                    ♦ Q 10 6
                    ♣ A 9 3 2
```

Contract: 4 ♥

Opening Lead: ♠ Ace

West led the top three spades. South ruffed the third round and tried to draw trumps. When they broke 4/2, he lost control of the hand and went down one.

Was there a way to keep control and scamper home with ten tricks?

3NT and five diamonds have no play, but four hearts can be made if declarer keeps control. In these situations, he must try to avoid ruffing himself into a 3/3 fit, discarding instead at Trick 3.

If West persists with a fourth spade, ruff in dummy, (the 3-card holding), draw trumps and enjoy your ten winners.

DEAL 63   PESKY 4/3 FIT

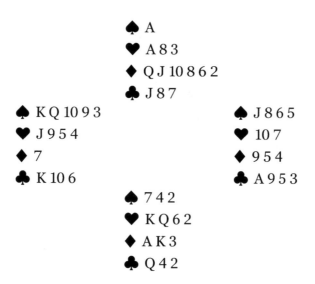

♠ A
♥ A 8 3
♦ Q J 10 8 6 2
♣ J 8 7

♠ K Q 10 9 3
♥ J 9 5 4
♦ 7
♣ K 10 6

♠ J 8 6 5
♥ 10 7
♦ 9 5 4
♣ A 9 5 3

♠ 7 4 2
♥ K Q 6 2
♦ A K 3
♣ Q 4 2

North	East	South	West
1♦	P	1♥	1♠
Dbl*	2♠	3♠	P
4♦	P	4♥	All Pass

* Support double, three hearts

Opening Lead: ♠ King

"Why aren't we in 3NT?" wondered South when he saw the dummy. As so many do, he immediately thought about ruffing spades in the dummy. (North tried unsuccessfully to stop him).

Declarer played a diamond to his hand and ruffed a spade. Even if he could return to ruff another spade, how would he draw trumps? A real mess.

If that line didn't work, how should you make four hearts?

You have a lot of tricks. Draw trumps and use them. But therein lies the catch. How to draw the trumps? The answer is easy. Assuming a 4/2 split, play low from both hands first.

Make them take their trump trick now. Then South can draw the rest and run the diamonds.

One spade, three hearts, and six diamonds. Easy game this bridge.

DEAL 64   THROW ANYTHING

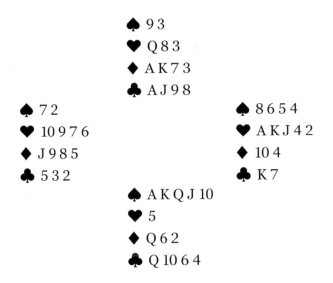

```
                    ♠ 9 3
                    ♥ Q 8 3
                    ♦ A K 7 3
                    ♣ A J 9 8
    ♠ 7 2                        ♠ 8 6 5 4
    ♥ 10 9 7 6                   ♥ A K J 4 2
    ♦ J 9 8 5                    ♦ 10 4
    ♣ 5 3 2                      ♣ K 7
                    ♠ A K Q J 10
                    ♥ 5
                    ♦ Q 6 2
                    ♣ Q 10 6 4
```

Contract: 4 ♠
Opening Lead: ♥ 10

Declarer ruffed the second heart and drew trumps, leaving himself with none. He cashed the top three diamonds.

But after taking a losing club finesse, he lost three more hearts. Well, that's the nine tricks he started with and the nine tricks he finished with.

What was the problem? How would you have handled all these assets?

The problem was losing control as usual, when trumps don't behave. Declarer can succeed with ease, ruffing the second heart and taking an early club finesse.

When East wins and returns a heart, declarer can throw virtually anything from his hand, low club, low diamond, low shoe. Another heart can now be ruffed in dummy. He then draws trumps and has the rest.

He loses two hearts and one club.

DEAL 65   PLENTY CAN GO WRONG

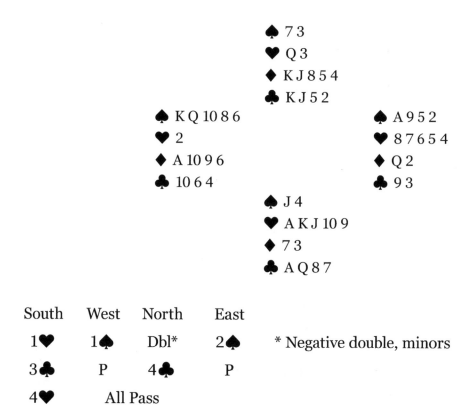

```
                    ♠ 7 3
                    ♥ Q 3
                    ♦ K J 8 5 4
                    ♣ K J 5 2
        ♠ K Q 10 8 6              ♠ A 9 5 2
        ♥ 2                       ♥ 8 7 6 5 4
        ♦ A 10 9 6                ♦ Q 2
        ♣ 10 6 4                  ♣ 9 3
                    ♠ J 4
                    ♥ A K J 10 9
                    ♦ 7 3
                    ♣ A Q 8 7
```

South	West	North	East
1♥	1♠	Dbl*	2♠	* Negative double, minors
3♣	P	4♣	P
4♥	All Pass

Opening Lead: ♠ King

The defense took two rounds of spades and East led a trump. Declarer cashed the A-K of trumps, West showed out. Declarer drew the trumps and cashed the clubs. But he couldn't play a diamond or the opponents would take their spades.

He ended with the same nine top tricks he started with. The diamond king is still sitting there as you read this. Down one.

Do you remember the song that starts "It's still the same old story?"

Another declarer saw the need to cater to a possible bad trump split. This is the principle of second suits first, leaving a trump in dummy.

Win Trick 3 and lead a diamond. Play West who bid for the ace. If West ducks, go up with the king. Now you have your tenth trick in the bag.

DEAL 66   KEEPING CONTROL

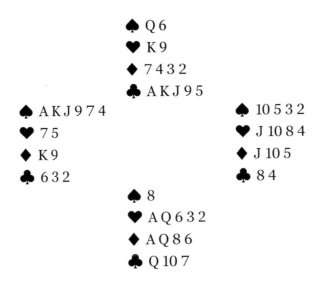

```
                    ♠ Q 6
                    ♥ K 9
                    ♦ 7 4 3 2
                    ♣ A K J 9 5
      ♠ A K J 9 7 4              ♠ 10 5 3 2
      ♥ 7 5                      ♥ J 10 8 4
      ♦ K 9                      ♦ J 10 5
      ♣ 6 3 2                    ♣ 8 4
                    ♠ 8
                    ♥ A Q 6 3 2
                    ♦ A Q 8 6
                    ♣ Q 10 7
```

Contract: 4 ♥

Opening Lead: ♠ Ace

South ruffed the second spade and started the trumps. West showed out on the third round. South stopped pulling trumps and started the clubs.

East ruffed the third club and returned a spade forcing out South's last trump.

Declarer's diamond ace was his last trick. Ugly.

Was there a better way to keep control of this hand?

Sure. If trumps were 3/3, eleven easy tricks. But to insure the contract, declarer should discard a diamond from his hand at Trick 2 rather than ruff.

What can the defense do? Another spade can be ruffed in the dummy. With a club shift South can win and take three high trumps.

After conceding one, he will have a trump left to take the rest.

DEAL 67   DO YOU RECOGNIZE ME?

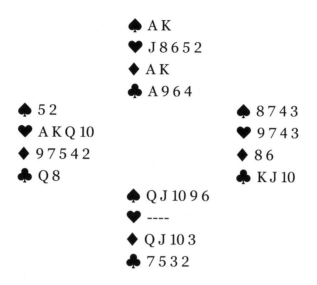

                    ♠ A K
                    ♥ J 8 6 5 2
                    ♦ A K
                    ♣ A 9 6 4

    ♠ 5 2   ♠ 8 7 4 3
    ♥ A K Q 10   ♥ 9 7 4 3
    ♦ 9 7 5 4 2   ♦ 8 6
    ♣ Q 8   ♣ K J 10

                    ♠ Q J 10 9 6
                    ♥ ----
                    ♦ Q J 10 3
                    ♣ 7 5 3 2

Contract: 4 ♠

Opening Lead: ♥ Ace

The first declarer saw no problem. He counted five spades, four diamonds, and one club, an easy game. He ruffed the opening lead, played the A-K of trumps and ruffed a heart back to his hand.

West showed out on the third round of trumps. Suddenly, maybe not so easy. East ruffed the third diamond and the hand fell apart.

Unlucky or a failure to recognize what the hand was all about?

Hand type recognition. Another declarer counted her tricks as follows: After ruffing the opening lead, she could cash two diamonds and one club. There were six more trump tricks, not five, available on a high crossruff.

The defenders could have the last three tricks, whatever was left over.

DEAL 68 MAINTAINING CONTROL IN THE 5/2 FIT

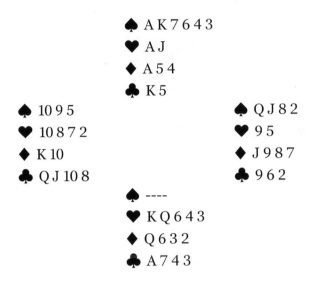

♠ A K 7 6 4 3
♥ A J
♦ A 5 4
♣ K 5

♠ 10 9 5
♥ 10 8 7 2
♦ K 10
♣ Q J 10 8

♠ Q J 8 2
♥ 9 5
♦ J 9 8 7
♣ 9 6 2

♠ ----
♥ K Q 6 4 3
♦ Q 6 3 2
♣ A 7 4 3

North	South
1♠	2♥
3♠	3NT
4NT	5NT
6♥	P

Opening Lead: ♣ Queen

Declarer won the opening lead with the ace and played two rounds of trumps. After cashing the A-K of spades, he ruffed a spade. He led a club to the king and ruffed another spade high.

Good news: The spades were 4/3. Bad news: When declarere played his last high trump, East showed out. He took one more trick, the diamond ace.
Down two.

Was there a way to set up the spades and keep control?

It's the old story; lose a trick early. After cashing two trumps, lead a low spade from dummy and discard something, (anything), just not a trump. Win the club return in dummy, ruff a spade and draw trumps.

The spades are good. Go to the diamond ace. Five trumps, four spades, one diamond, and two clubs. It's an easy game. Thanks to Frank Stewart for this one.

DEAL 69   GET INSURANCE BEFORE, NOT AFTER THE ACCIDENT

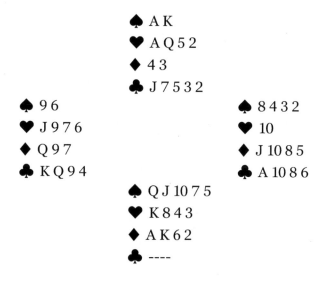

```
                    ♠ A K
                    ♥ A Q 5 2
                    ♦ 4 3
                    ♣ J 7 5 3 2
       ♠ 9 6                         ♠ 8 4 3 2
       ♥ J 9 7 6                     ♥ 10
       ♦ Q 9 7                       ♦ J 10 8 5
       ♣ K Q 9 4                     ♣ A 10 8 6
                    ♠ Q J 10 7 5
                    ♥ K 8 4 3
                    ♦ A K 6 2
                    ♣ ----
```

Contract: 6 ♥

Opening Lead: ♣ King

"Thanks partner," South said, thinking thirteen tricks, and he quickly cashed the A-K of trumps. When East discarded on the second trump, play slowed. "Great," thought North, knowing what had probably happened, another cold slam going down.

South tried to recover. He ruffed another club, cashed the A-K of spades, a diamond to his ace and led a spade hoping to discard clubs. West ruffed and cashed the clubs. Down two. "Very nice," thought North.

How should declarer play (besides slower)?

The contract is six hearts, not seven. Only a 4/1 trump split can jeopardize the slam. As usual, lose one early. Play a low trump from both hands at Trick 2.

Win the return, say a diamond, with the ace, then a spade to dummy and ruff a club. Then the king of trumps, the king of spades, draw trumps, a diamond to the king and run the spades in leisure. Twelve tricks.

DEAL 70 DRAWING TRUMPS AND KEEPING CONTROL

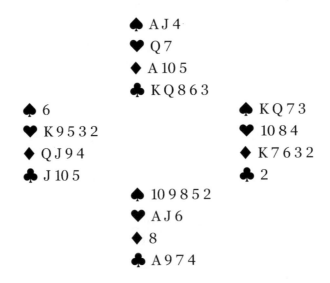

♠ A J 4
♥ Q 7
♦ A 10 5
♣ K Q 8 6 3

♠ 6
♥ K 9 5 3 2
♦ Q J 9 4
♣ J 10 5

♠ K Q 7 3
♥ 10 8 4
♦ K 7 6 3 2
♣ 2

♠ 10 9 8 5 2
♥ A J 6
♦ 8
♣ A 9 7 4

Contract: 4 ♠

Opening Lead: ♦ Queen

Declarer won the opening lead, but there was danger lurking. This was an exercise in keeping control while skirting a variety of problems. Taking spade finesses could open the door to a club ruff.

But cashing the spade ace would allow an opponent with ♠KQxx to take over with repeated diamond forces. After taking forever, declarer finished down one.

What's the best line to keep control on the way to ten tricks?

Hard to see but try leading the spade jack at Trick 2. Ruff the diamond return and duck another trump. Of course, trumps are 4/1.

If the defense persists with another diamond, discard a heart, and win the (say) heart return with the ace. Another diamond can be ruffed in dummy.

Unblock the spade ace and play a club to the ace. Draw the last trump. You have five clubs, three spades and two aces. Very nice!

DEAL 71   OTHER BUSINESS

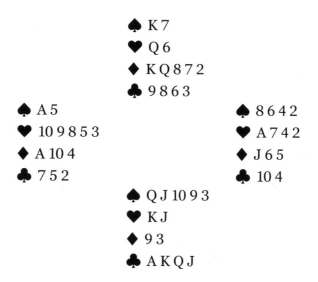

                    ♠ K 7
                    ♥ Q 6
                    ♦ K Q 8 7 2
                    ♣ 9 8 6 3

    ♠ A 5   ♠ 8 6 4 2
    ♥ 10 9 8 5 3   ♥ A 7 4 2
    ♦ A 10 4   ♦ J 6 5
    ♣ 7 5 2   ♣ 10 4

                    ♠ Q J 10 9 3
                    ♥ K J
                    ♦ 9 3
                    ♣ A K Q J

Contract: 4 ♠

Opening Lead: ♥ 10

East won the opening lead and returned a heart. Declarer won and started to draw trumps. West won the second trump and returned another heart.

Declarer ruffed and when trumps were 4/1, had none left when she had to finally play a diamond. Down one.

How can you make four spades?

Since declarer needs one diamond trick, lead a diamond at Trick 3 while there are still trumps in dummy to handle the repeated attacks in hearts.

With one, or two diamond tricks in the bank, go about your business, scoring four spades, four clubs, one heart, and at least one diamond.

DEAL 72   DANGER LURKS AGAIN

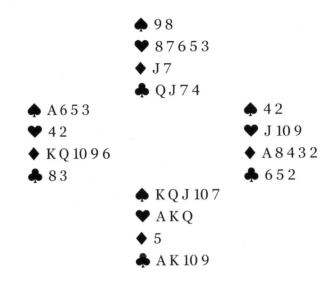

♠ 9 8
♥ 8 7 6 5 3
♦ J 7
♣ Q J 7 4

♠ A 6 5 3
♥ 4 2
♦ K Q 10 9 6
♣ 8 3

♠ 4 2
♥ J 10 9
♦ A 8 4 3 2
♣ 6 5 2

♠ K Q J 10 7
♥ A K Q
♦ 5
♣ A K 10 9

Contract: 4 ♠ (East and West bid diamonds)
Opening Lead: ♦ King

Even with such a strong looking suit, trouble lurks. Declarer ruffed the second diamond and started trumps. West won the second round and continued diamonds, leaving West with two trumps and declarer with one.

Bye-bye. Declarer lost control and went down.

How would you have maintained control?

To avoid being "tapped out," declarer must refuse to ruff at Trick 2. He doesn't really have a loser to discard, but he must throw something, perhaps a lavish ace of hearts or clubs.

The next diamond can be ruffed in the dummy and the contract is safe.

Note that at the first table, West made a good play of winning the second round of trumps. If she wins the first, declarer can ruff a diamond return in the dummy.

DEAL 73   CAREFULLY PRESERVED

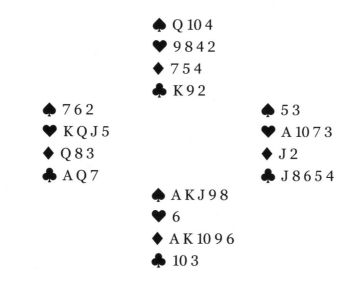

```
                        ♠ Q 10 4
                        ♥ 9 8 4 2
                        ♦ 7 5 4
                        ♣ K 9 2
        ♠ 7 6 2                         ♠ 5 3
        ♥ K Q J 5                       ♥ A 10 7 3
        ♦ Q 8 3                         ♦ J 2
        ♣ A Q 7                         ♣ J 8 6 5 4
                        ♠ A K J 9 8
                        ♥ 6
                        ♦ A K 10 9 6
                        ♣ 10 3
```

South	West	North	East
1♠	Dbl	P	2♥
3♦	P	3♠	P
4♠	All Pass		

Opening Lead: ♥ King

Declarer ruffed the second heart. After drawing three rounds of trumps, he played the A-K of diamonds and gave up a diamond. The heart return took his last trump. He still had to lose a club and a heart. Down one.

How might declarer have kept better control to make four spades?

When control is uncertain, establishment of side suits or vital tricks before drawing trumps is often key. Declarer needs the club king to make the contract so he should lead a club at Trick 3. West wins and returns another heart. South can ruff but should draw only two rounds of trumps and concede a diamond.

But viva la difference. Yes, he is forced to ruff the heart return with the last trump in his hand but he can go to the club king in dummy. Now he can draw the last trump with the "carefully preserved" queen and run the diamonds.

The principle of trying to keep at least one trump in each hand makes life much easier.

81

DEAL 74   THROWING STUFF AWAY

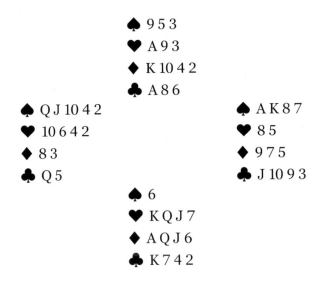

♠ 9 5 3
♥ A 9 3
♦ K 10 4 2
♣ A 8 6

♠ Q J 10 4 2
♥ 10 6 4 2
♦ 8 3
♣ Q 5

♠ A K 8 7
♥ 8 5
♦ 9 7 5
♣ J 10 9 3

♠ 6
♥ K Q J 7
♦ A Q J 6
♣ K 7 4 2

Contract: 4 ♥
Opening Lead: ♠ Queen

Declarer ruffed the second spade and tried drawing trumps, hoping for a 3-3 trump split. He was quickly out of trumps after the three rounds.

North was muttering under his breath things I can't print while E/W were figuring out the undertricks.

What do you think North was saying?

It's difficult to sit quietly watching partner go down in a cold game. Declarer should discard a club at Trick 2. When the defense continued spades, what should declarer do?

Yes, throw another club. And then no, do not throw any more clubs, claim.

Making four hearts.

SAVING AND CREATING ENTRIES

DEAL 75   ENTRIES, ENTRIES, ENTRIES

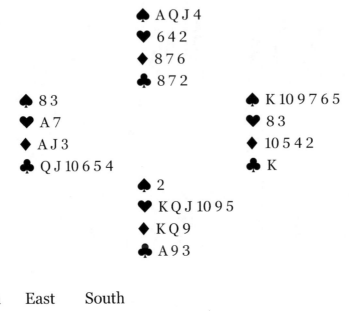

♠ A Q J 4
♥ 6 4 2
♦ 8 7 6
♣ 8 7 2

♠ 8 3
♥ A 7
♦ A J 3
♣ Q J 10 6 5 4

♠ K 10 9 7 6 5
♥ 8 3
♦ 10 5 4 2
♣ K

♠ 2
♥ K Q J 10 9 5
♦ K Q 9
♣ A 9 3

West	North	East	South
1♣	P	1♠	2♥
P	P	2♠	3♥
All Pass			

Opening Lead: ♣ Queen

Declarer won the first trick and started the trumps. West won the ace and cashed two rounds of clubs, East discarding spades. West exited a trump, East following. Declarer led a spade to the ace and returned a diamond.

But with East likely have the spade king, West was sure to have the diamond ace. West won and returned a diamond. Declarer ended down one.

Do you see a way to take nine tricks?

Declarer can lead a spade to the ace, but then lead the queen of spades. When East covers, ruff and return to dummy to cash the good spade jack.

What no entry? Please don't tell me you ruffed the spade with the heart five.

DEAL 76   NEED AN ENTRY? MAKE AN OFFER

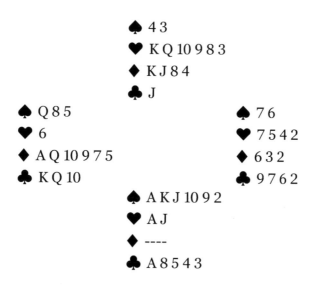

```
                    ♠ 4 3
                    ♥ K Q 10 9 8 3
                    ♦ K J 8 4
                    ♣ J
        ♠ Q 8 5                      ♠ 7 6
        ♥ 6                          ♥ 7 5 4 2
        ♦ A Q 10 9 7 5               ♦ 6 3 2
        ♣ K Q 10                     ♣ 9 7 6 2
                    ♠ A K J 10 9 2
                    ♥ A J
                    ♦ ----
                    ♣ A 8 5 4 3
```

Contract: 6 ♠
Opening Lead: ♣ King

Declarer wanted to throw all her losers on the good hearts in dummy, but she had no entry. She hopefully tried cashing the A-K of trumps; if the queen falls she could draw the last trump and overtake in hearts. Of course, that's only in her dreams.

Any thoughts?

Sure, make the opponents an offer they cannot refuse. Start with the jack, or even better the nine of trumps. Game, set, and match.

If West wins the queen, there is still a trump in dummy. And looking at the nine, he might even duck! Only if spades are 4/1 and that player ducks are you going down. Or if one player can now ruff a heart.

That would really be, as Eddie Kantar said, "The winner of the saddest bridge story of the year."

DEAL 77   MORE 4/1 PROBLEMS: LACK OF ENTRIES

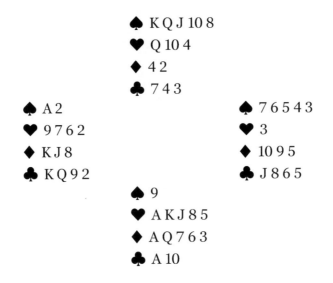

♠ K Q J 10 8
♥ Q 10 4
♦ 4 2
♣ 7 4 3

♠ A 2   ♠ 7 6 5 4 3
♥ 9 7 6 2   ♥ 3
♦ K J 8   ♦ 10 9 5
♣ K Q 9 2   ♣ J 8 6 5

♠ 9
♥ A K J 8 5
♦ A Q 7 6 3
♣ A 10

Contract: 4 ♥

Opening Lead: ♣ King

Declarer won the club ace and cashed the ace of hearts. He led a spade. West won the ace and continued clubs forcing South to ruff. South now played the heart king, not thinking about what might go wrong. East showed him.

Declarer continued a heart to the queen and started the spades. But West ruffed the third spade and played another club. With two diamond losers, declarer was down one.

Not an easy hand. Was there a way to overcome the 4/1 split?

Ask yourself what could go wrong. The only thing, of course, would be a 4/1 trump split. So instead of the heart king, lead to the heart ten. If both follow, all is fine.

Now continue spades, letting West ruff in when he liked. Win the return, and with a heart to the queen you have the rest.

DEAL 78 IMPROVING THE ODDS

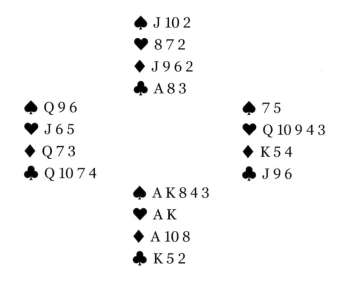

♠ J 10 2
♥ 8 7 2
♦ J 9 6 2
♣ A 8 3

♠ Q 9 6
♥ J 6 5
♦ Q 7 3
♣ Q 10 7 4

♠ 7 5
♥ Q 10 9 4 3
♦ K 5 4
♣ J 9 6

♠ A K 8 4 3
♥ A K
♦ A 10 8
♣ K 5 2

Contract: 4 ♠

Opening Lead: ♣ 4

With four possible losers, declarer won the club ace and took a trump finesse, losing (they always lose in the books). A club came back.

Now declarer needed a very unlikely diamond position and went down one.

Was there a better percentage play for game?

Let's say the trump finesse is roughly 50%. Split diamond honors offer a 75% chance, but you need two entries. Try winning the club lead in hand, cash one high trump and lead a low one.

Now with two dummy entries, all you need is one diamond honor onside, losing one diamond, one trump, and one club. Better odds.

DEAL 79   SACRIFICE TO CREATE AN ENTRY

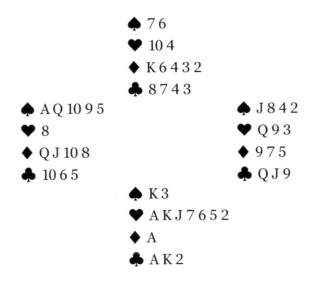

```
                    ♠ 7 6
                    ♥ 10 4
                    ♦ K 6 4 3 2
                    ♣ 8 7 4 3
     ♠ A Q 10 9 5                    ♠ J 8 4 2
     ♥ 8                             ♥ Q 9 3
     ♦ Q J 10 8                      ♦ 9 7 5
     ♣ 10 6 5                        ♣ Q J 9
                    ♠ K 3
                    ♥ A K J 7 6 5 2
                    ♦ A
                    ♣ A K 2
```

Contract: 4 ♥

Opening Lead: ♦ Queen

Declarer won the opening lead perforce and hopefully cashed the A-K of trumps. Since the queen did not fall, the diamond king is still sitting in the dummy as you are reading this book. The declarer also lost two spades and a club, down one.

Do you see any way to rescue the diamond king?

Again you need to create an entry. Try leading the heart jack at Trick 2. The good news first. If hearts are 2/2 or 3/1, the opponents will have to win the queen or lose it. The club loser can now go away on the diamond king.

The potential bad news. If West has four hearts and lets the jack hold, cash the A-K of hearts, the A-K of clubs and exit a heart. If West started with less than three clubs, he will have to lead a diamond or spade giving you a tenth trick.

If East started with four hearts, please go on to the next page.

DEAL 80 CAN TRUMPS BE ENTRIES?

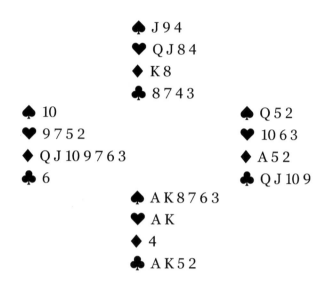

♠ J 9 4
♥ Q J 8 4
♦ K 8
♣ 8 7 4 3

♠ 10
♥ 9 7 5 2
♦ Q J 10 9 7 6 3
♣ 6

♠ Q 5 2
♥ 10 6 3
♦ A 5 2
♣ Q J 10 9

♠ A K 8 7 6 3
♥ A K
♦ 4
♣ A K 5 2

South	West	North	East
2♣	3♦	P	4♦
4♠	5♦	5♠	All Pass

Opening Lead: ♦ Queen

South ruffed the second diamond and played the spade ace. West played the ten. South hopefully cashed the spade king but of course West showed out.

Now South had no entry to the hearts. South ended up losing a spade and two clubs, down two.

Was there a road to making five spades against any distribution?

Declarer should cash the A-K of hearts before playing any more trumps. If these win, then just lead a low spade, no matter the spade layout. Now South has a trump entry to the good hearts to discard clubs.

If one of the heart honors gets ruffed, it doesn't matter. That would leave only one remaining trump.

DEAL 81   TRUMPS ARE YOUR ONLY ENTRIES

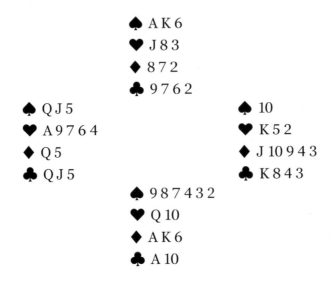

♠ A K 6
♥ J 8 3
♦ 8 7 2
♣ 9 7 6 2

♠ Q J 5
♥ A 9 7 6 4
♦ Q 5
♣ Q J 5

♠ 10
♥ K 5 2
♦ J 10 9 4 3
♣ K 8 4 3

♠ 9 8 7 4 3 2
♥ Q 10
♦ A K 6
♣ A 10

Contract: 3 ♠

Opening Lead: ♣ Queen

Declarer has possibly ten tricks if everything goes well. But he is in three, not four spades. He won the opening lead, cashed the A-K of trumps and when they were 3/1, lost two hearts, one spade, one club, and one diamond.

Forget ten tricks, what happened to nine?

Was there a way to survive the bad trump break?

Of course. Poor timing. Declarer needs to try to set up a heart trick and the trump suit is his only entry. At Trick 2, lead a heart. Now he is ahead in the race.

When he gets in, one round of trumps and another heart. Now the heart in dummy is good and you have a trump as an entry.

DEAL 82   MR. CRAFTY

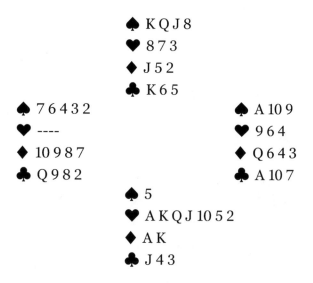

Contract: 4 ♥

Opening Lead: ♦ 10

Declarer won the opening lead, drew trumps and led a spade. Unable to reach dummy, he had to play clubs himself, down one. The good spades are still there.

A crafty declarer found a way to use the spades. How?

When you play golf and say you got a par on a hole, no one asks you how. It's how many. It's the same in bridge. If you make your contract, like four hearts, no one cares which three tricks you lost, only that you made it.

The crafty declarer won the opening diamond and played one round of trumps. When West showed out played a spade. East won and returned a diamond.

Declarer now led a LOW heart giving East the lead. The heart eight was the entry to the spades. Mr. Crafty lost one spade, one club, and one unexpected heart.

A par is a par.

DEAL 83   A LITTLE DECEPTION TO
FIND A NEEDED ENTRY

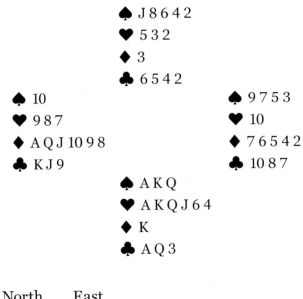

♠ J 8 6 4 2
♥ 5 3 2
♦ 3
♣ 6 5 4 2

♠ 10
♥ 9 8 7
♦ A Q J 10 9 8
♣ K J 9

♠ 9 7 5 3
♥ 10
♦ 7 6 5 4 2
♣ 10 8 7

♠ A K Q
♥ A K Q J 6 4
♦ K
♣ A Q 3

South	West	North	East
2♣	3♦	P	5♦
5♥	All Pass		

Opening Lead: ♦ Ace

West led the diamond ace and switched to the heart nine. Declarer cashed another high trump, East showed out, so there was no entry to dummy.

Declare lost two clubs. Down one. Too bad, such a nice hand, but those obnoxious opponents pushed you too high.

How can South make five hearts?

A little swindle. Always be wary of gifts from good players. Declarer, after cashing one high trump, played the A-K of spades. East ruffed. Pretty hard play to see that ruffing was wrong.

Voila! Declarer now had an entry after drawing the last trump, the heart four, to get to dummy and use all those nice spades.

DEAL 84   CAREFULLY PRESERVED
IS CAREFULLY PRESERVED

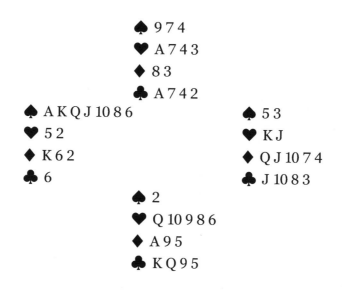

```
                    ♠ 9 7 4
                    ♥ A 7 4 3
                    ♦ 8 3
                    ♣ A 7 4 2
♠ A K Q J 10 8 6                    ♠ 5 3
♥ 5 2                               ♥ K J
♦ K 6 2                             ♦ Q J 10 7 4
♣ 6                                 ♣ J 10 8 3
                    ♠ 2
                    ♥ Q 10 9 8 6
                    ♦ A 9 5
                    ♣ K Q 9 5
```

South	West	North	East
1♥	3♠	4♥	All Pass

Opening Lead: ♠ Ace

Declarer ruffed the second spade. He led a trump to the ace and a trump back. East won and returned a diamond. Declarer ducked, won the next diamond and ruffed his last diamond.

After ruffing another spade, declarer knew West had started with seven spades, three diamonds and two hearts. He led a club to dummy and returned a club. East played the ten, declarer won the queen.

Declarer still had the ♣K9 over East's ♣J8, but he had no way to reach dummy for another club finesse. Down one.

How did the declarer at the other table make four hearts?

Eddie Kantar is credited with the term "the carefully preserved two." But it can be the carefully preserved almost anything. Just try to get in the habit if possible of not ruffing with your lowest trump.

If you still have the trump six, to reach the seven in dummy, you can finesse East out of his club winner and make your contract.

The carefully preserved six, right Eddie?

DEAL 85   TRUMP ENTRIES

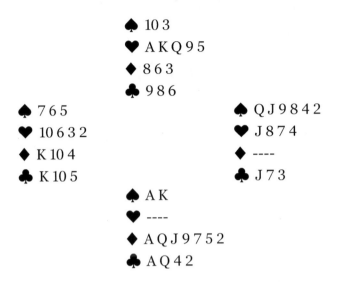

♠ 10 3
♥ A K Q 9 5
♦ 8 6 3
♣ 9 8 6

♠ 7 6 5
♥ 10 6 3 2
♦ K 10 4
♣ K 10 5

♠ Q J 9 8 4 2
♥ J 8 7 4
♦ ----
♣ J 7 3

♠ A K
♥ ----
♦ A Q J 9 7 5 2
♣ A Q 4 2

East	South	West	North
2♠	5♦		All Pass

Opening Lead: ♠ 5

This hand was originally played on BBO and reported by Mike Lawrence (ACBL Bulletin, January, 2018). The declarer, unable to reach those nice hearts in dummy, led the diamond ace at Trick 2, East showing out.

There was no recourse, declarer losing one diamond and two clubs.

Is there a better line of play?

A 3/0 split is not uncommon, about 22% of the time. To create an entry to the hearts to dump the clubs, lead a low diamond at Trick 2. If trumps are 2/1, you can pick up the king next time and the diamond eight is an entry.

Even with a 3/0 trump split, win the return, another low diamond and West has to take his king or lose it. That eight is still there to get to the hearts.
Declarer loses two trump tricks, but no clubs.

DEAL 86   SPEEDING TICKET

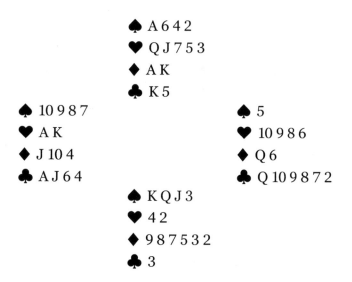

```
              ♠ A 6 4 2
              ♥ Q J 7 5 3
              ♦ A K
              ♣ K 5
♠ 10 9 8 7                    ♠ 5
♥ A K                         ♥ 10 9 8 6
♦ J 10 4                      ♦ Q 6
♣ A J 6 4                     ♣ Q 10 9 8 7 2
              ♠ K Q J 3
              ♥ 4 2
              ♦ 9 8 7 5 3 2
              ♣ 3
```

North   South

1♥   1♠

4♠   P

Opening Lead: ♠ 10

Declarer too quickly played low from dummy, winning in hand. The diamonds looked like the best source of tricks.

But even after finding a 3/2 diamond split, and West with three, declarer was unable to both draw trumps, ruff one diamond and return to his hand.

Where did declarer go wrong?

Declarer is going to need entries to his hand and some luck. Win Trick 1 with the ace of trumps. Now the rest is the same.

He is able to ruff a diamond in dummy, West having to follow. He can get back to his hand and draw all the trumps. The diamonds are good.

DEAL 87   I KNOW YOU

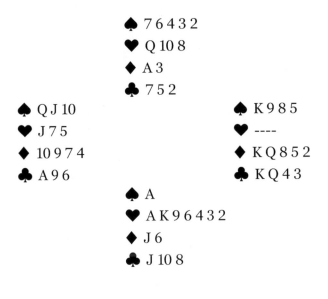

♠ 7 6 4 3 2
♥ Q 10 8
♦ A 3
♣ 7 5 2

♠ Q J 10
♥ J 7 5
♦ 10 9 7 4
♣ A 9 6

♠ K 9 8 5
♥ ----
♦ K Q 8 5 2
♣ K Q 4 3

♠ A
♥ A K 9 6 4 3 2
♦ J 6
♣ J 10 8

South	West	North	East
1♥	P	2♥	Dbl
4♥		All Pass	

Opening Lead: ♠ Queen

Declarer won the opening lead. It looked grim; if his minors were reversed, he could have ruffed a third diamond. He went down one quietly.

How did an other declarer make four hearts?

Hand pattern recognition is what a declarer should always be thinking about. What kind of hand is this? Well, a second suit is a second suit. You only need length, not quality. But you do need entries. And this hand seems one entry shy even if spades are 4/3. But declarer saw a ray of hope.

Hey, if you go down, it's only one more undertrick. At Trick 2, she played a trump to dummy's eight! It won, East showing out. Now ruff a spade high, lead a trump to the ten, ruff another spade high, another trump to dummy drawing the last trump.

One more spade ruff and the last spade is good. The diamond ace is still there as an entry and you can discard your diamond loser. It never hurts to try, but recognizing the hand type first is key.

DEAL 88   EARLY OR LATER, IT'S ALL THE SAME

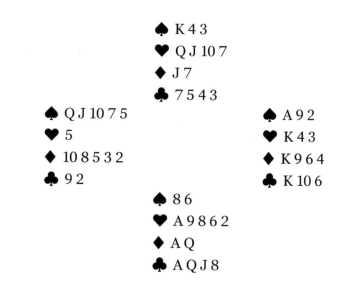

♠ K 4 3
♥ Q J 10 7
♦ J 7
♣ 7 5 4 3

♠ Q J 10 7 5
♥ 5
♦ 10 8 5 3 2
♣ 9 2

♠ A 9 2
♥ K 4 3
♦ K 9 6 4
♣ K 10 6

♠ 8 6
♥ A 9 8 6 2
♦ A Q
♣ A Q J 8

East	South	West	North
1♦	1♥	P	2♥
P	4♥	All Pass	

Opening Lead: ♠ Queen

Declarer ruffed the third round of spades. She had three finesses which rated to win but she lacked entries. Declarer tried leading the heart ace, both followed low, and a low trump. East won and returned a trump.

Declarer now had two entries but needed three to pick up both minor kings. Down one.

How did another declarer find another entry?

Since declarer saw the hand the same way, (the finesses rating to win), she ruffed the third spade with the ace of trumps. This looks like an extra loser, but it's a trick declarer expected to lose anyhow.

By losing it early, she had three entries to dummy. Making four hearts.

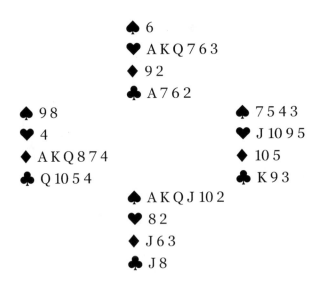

North	East	South	West
1♥	P	1♠	2♦
3♥	P	4♠	All Pass

Opening Lead: ♦ Ace

West played the A-K of diamonds, East playing the ten and five. When West continued with the queen, declarer ruffed and East overruffed. East returned a club setting up a trick for the defense.

Declarer was in trouble. He could not reach his hand to draw trumps and he could not use the hearts because West would ruff in.

Down one, sad with all those tricks.

Did this have to happen?

This theme was in a bridge column by Barry Rigal and shown by Michael Lawrence. It was simple: Just let West have his queen of diamonds.

Declarer can win the next trick and he has a trump entry to his hand.

DEAL 90   GO SLOW

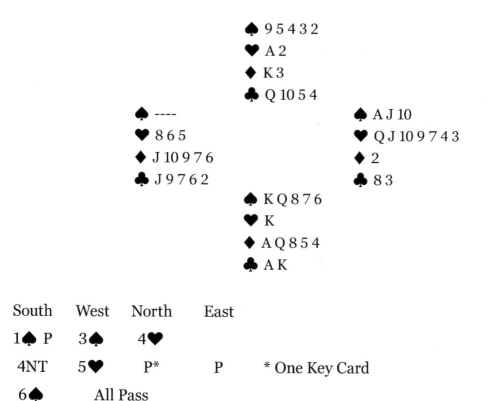

```
                    ♠ 9 5 4 3 2
                    ♥ A 2
                    ♦ K 3
                    ♣ Q 10 5 4
        ♠ ----                      ♠ A J 10
        ♥ 8 6 5                     ♥ Q J 10 9 7 4 3
        ♦ J 10 9 7 6                ♦ 2
        ♣ J 9 7 6 2                 ♣ 8 3
                    ♠ K Q 8 7 6
                    ♥ K
                    ♦ A Q 8 5 4
                    ♣ A K
```

South	West	North	East
1♠ P	3♠	4♥	
4NT	5♥	P*	P	* One Key Card
6♠	All Pass		

Opening Lead: ♥ 8

South, too quickly, won the king in hand. He played a diamond to the king and led a trump. East played the ten, declarer the king, West showed out.

Trying to get back to dummy, declarer played ace of diamonds, East ruffed. Down one.

Careless, greedy, or just playing too quickly?

Probably too quickly. If only the heart king had been a deuce. Another declarer saw the key was to just draw trumps.

She won the ace at Trick 1 and started the trumps. Now she still had the one necessary entry to "do it again."

DEAL 91   TIMING

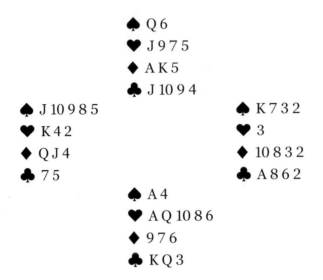

♠ Q 6
♥ J 9 7 5
♦ A K 5
♣ J 10 9 4

♠ J 10 9 8 5   ♠ K 7 3 2
♥ K 4 2   ♥ 3
♦ Q J 4   ♦ 10 8 3 2
♣ 7 5   ♣ A 8 6 2

♠ A 4
♥ A Q 10 8 6
♦ 9 7 6
♣ K Q 3

Contract: 4 ♥
Opening Lead: ♠ Jack

The first trick went queen, king, ace. Declarer crossed to the ace of diamonds to take the trump finesse. West won the king, cashed the spade ten and returned the diamond queen.

When East won the club ace, she returned a diamond to West for the setting trick.

What should declarer have done?

Declarer should realize the heart finesse was an illusion. There were ten tricks, even if the trump finesse was wrong. One spade, four hearts, two diamonds, and three clubs, provided South keeps his dummy entries.

Just draw trumps by starting with the ace. This gives declarer the tempo and entries to set up the clubs and take ten tricks.

DEAL 92   DON'T BE CHEAP

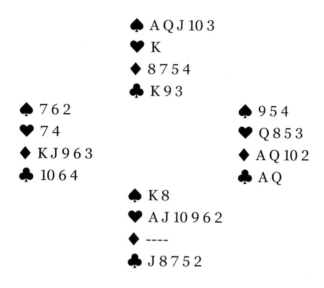

♠ A Q J 10 3
♥ K
♦ 8 7 5 4
♣ K 9 3

♠ 7 6 2
♥ 7 4
♦ K J 9 6 3
♣ 10 6 4

♠ 9 5 4
♥ Q 8 5 3
♦ A Q 10 2
♣ A Q

♠ K 8
♥ A J 10 9 6 2
♦ ----
♣ J 8 7 5 2

East	South	West	North
1♦	1♥	3♦	3♠
P	4♥		All Pass

Opening Lead: ♦ 6

Declarer ruffed the opening lead and led a trump to the king. He came to his hand with the spade king to play the A-J of trumps. East won and returned a spade. Declarer now realized his problem; he was "locked" in the dummy.

Maybe he should have thought of that sooner?

He tried to cash two more spades, but East ruffed the second spade. Declarer overruffed and played a club. East won and made declarer ruff another diamond with his last trump. Down two.

How would you have managed to untangle the hand?

Start the trumps with the ace (who needs the king?) and continued with the jack. Now you have control. Ruff the diamond return and draw trumps.

The spades were untouched and there for the taking.

DRAW TRUMPS ?

YES OR NO ?

DRAWING TRUMPS: WHERE TO START?

The opening lead takes away your only dummy entry. But you want to pull trumps.

♠ A 6 3

♠ Q J 5 4 2

You can afford to lose one trick. How to handle this combination?

                     ♠ A 6 3

♠ 8   ♠ K 10 9 7

                     ♠ Q J 5 4 2

Lead low towards the Q J, hoping East has the king. Do NOT cash the ace first. If East happens to hold four trumps including the king, it will be necessary to lead a second time towards our hand.

We lead to the queen and it wins the trick. We return to the ace, West showing out and we are in the dummy to lead towards our jack. We escape for one trump loser.

Both the inferior plays of cashing the spade ace on the first round or leading the queen from our hand would result in losing two tricks as the cards lie. When trumps break 3/2, any play will succeed.

Of course, if West held four trumps including the king, no play would succeed.

WHICH CARD TO LEAD TO FINESSE?

♠ 10 4 3 2

♠ ?   ♠ ?

♠ A J 9 7

Assuming plenty of entries, how should declarer play this trump suit?

It's best to start low to the jack, not to lead the ten from dummy. Why?

If the layout is 4/1:

♠ K 8 6 5   ♠ Q

Whenever East has a singleton honor, you will lose an extra trump trick to West.

After the first finesse loses, now is the time to lead the 10. If West has the singleton honor:

♠ K   ♠ Q 8 6 5

Now by leading the ten and either running it if East ducks, or winning your ace if he covers, you are left with 9-7 in hand over his 8-6, and you can take a further finesse

DEAL 93   DRAW TRUMPS? YES AND NO

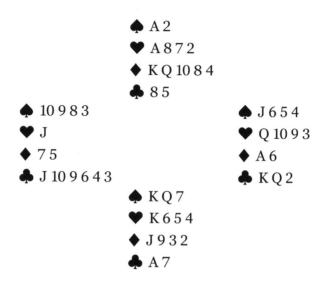

♠ A 2
♥ A 8 7 2
♦ K Q 10 8 4
♣ 8 5

♠ 10 9 8 3
♥ J
♦ 7 5
♣ J 10 9 6 4 3

♠ J 6 5 4
♥ Q 10 9 3
♦ A 6
♣ K Q 2

♠ K Q 7
♥ K 6 5 4
♦ J 9 3 2
♣ A 7

Contract: 4 ♥

Opening Lead: ♣ Jack

Mike Lawrence says millions of contracts have gone down, because either 1) declarer drew trumps too quickly, or 2) he waited too long to draw them.

Here is an example of what not to do.

South won the club lead and played three rounds of spades, discarding the club loser. Then South played the A-K of trumps.

Needing diamond tricks, South led the diamond king. East won, drew all the trumps and took the rest of the tricks. Not a good result, four hearts was cold.

What was a better way to avoid this disaster? What would Mike say?

Always make sure you can afford to draw trumps or at least how many you should draw. On this hand, declarer, after getting rid of the club loser can play one high trump and then start the diamonds.

Worst case scenario, they get a diamond ruff. You can handle it from there. When declarer gets back in, now the other high trump and more and more diamonds.

South loses only two trumps and one diamond.

DEAL 94   DRAWING TRUMPS?

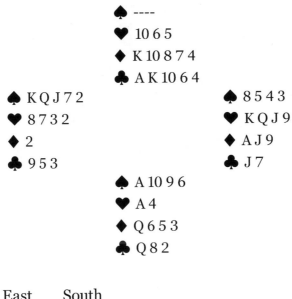

```
                    ♠ ----
                    ♥ 10 6 5
                    ♦ K 10 8 7 4
                    ♣ A K 10 6 4
   ♠ K Q J 7 2                      ♠ 8 5 4 3
   ♥ 8 7 3 2                        ♥ K Q J 9
   ♦ 2                              ♦ A J 9
   ♣ 9 5 3                          ♣ J 7
                    ♠ A 10 9 6
                    ♥ A 4
                    ♦ Q 6 5 3
                    ♣ Q 8 2
```

West	North	East	South
P	P	1♥	Dbl
2♠	4NT	P	5♦
All Pass			

Opening Lead: ♠ King

Declarer discarded a heart, winning the spade ace. He led a diamond to the ten and East's jack. East played the heart king. South finished down one.

Was there a better line of play?

It's usually better to ruff the first trick in these situations. On the bidding, East is likely to have the ace of trumps. Ruff the opening lead and play one round of trumps. East has to duck.

OK, that's enough trumps for now. South starts the clubs not caring if the third round is ruffed. East ruffs with the jack and switches belatedly to hearts. South wins, ruffs another spade and plays a fourth round of clubs discarding his heart loser. East is welcome to his diamond ace.

Note the importance of leading the first diamond from dummy, preventing East from winning with the ace except at the cost of a trick.

DEAL 95   DRAW TRUMPS? ENTRY PROBLEMS

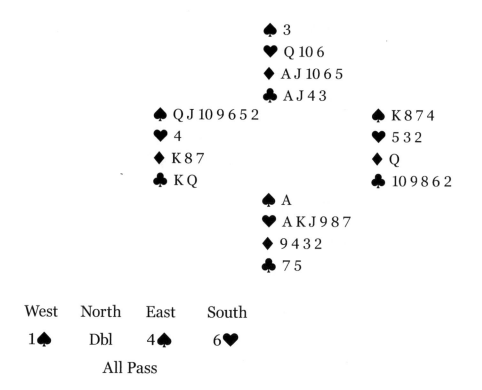

♠ 3
♥ Q 10 6
♦ A J 10 6 5
♣ A J 4 3

♠ Q J 10 9 6 5 2
♥ 4
♦ K 8 7
♣ K Q

♠ K 8 7 4
♥ 5 3 2
♦ Q
♣ 10 9 8 6 2

♠ A
♥ A K J 9 8 7
♦ 9 4 3 2
♣ 7 5

West	North	East	South
1♠	Dbl	4♠	6♥
	All Pass		

Opening Lead: ♠ Queen

Declarer won the opening lead. He drew trumps which were 3/1 and took a diamond finesse losing to the queen. East returned a club. With no way back to his hand, declarer cashed the diamond ace.

When the king didn't fall, he was down one.

How should he have handled the slam?

The correct way to play the diamond suit, ♦9432 facing ♦AJ1065 is to take two finesses. But declarer needed entries. He can afford to draw two rounds of trumps, but he must postpone the last round.

He needs the last trump as the entry to repeat the diamond finesse.

DEAL 96   TRUMP MANAGEMENT

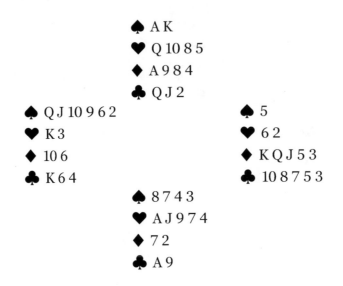

♠ A K
♥ Q 10 8 5
♦ A 9 8 4
♣ Q J 2

♠ Q J 10 9 6 2
♥ K 3
♦ 10 6
♣ K 6 4

♠ 5
♥ 6 2
♦ K Q J 5 3
♣ 10 8 7 5 3

♠ 8 7 4 3
♥ A J 9 7 4
♦ 7 2
♣ A 9

West	North	East	South
2♠	Dbl	P	3♥
P	4♥	All Pass	

Opening Lead: ♠ Queen

Declarer won the opening lead and took a trump finesse. West won the king and played another spade. East ruffed.

When the club finesse lost, declarer was down one.

Unlucky or greedy?

Maybe both, but declarer should give West some high cards since the ♠AK are in the dummy. East almost certainly has a singleton spade.

Declarer should simply start the trumps from the top to assure his contract, maybe with an overtrick. Who knows?

DEAL 97   EVELYN DRAWS THE TRUMPS

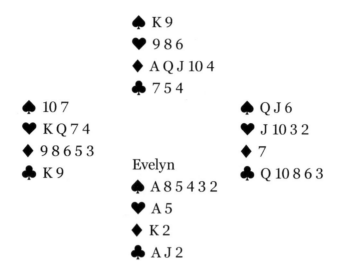

                    ♠ K 9
                    ♥ 9 8 6
                    ♦ A Q J 10 4
                    ♣ 7 5 4

♠ 10 7   ♠ Q J 6
♥ K Q 7 4   ♥ J 10 3 2
♦ 9 8 6 5 3   Evelyn   ♦ 7
♣ K 9   ♣ Q 10 8 6 3

                    ♠ A 8 5 4 3 2
                    ♥ A 5
                    ♦ K 2
                    ♣ A J 2

Contract: 4 ♠
Opening Lead: ♥ King

The infamous Evelyn, one of my students, won the opening lead and played the king, then ace of spades. Both opponents followed. Seeing that she could throw her losers on the diamonds, she played the diamond king, then led a low diamond. East ruffed and you know the rest of the story.

But she complained to me "You always tell me not to play more trumps when there is just one high one left."

How would you have responded to her lament?

Bridge is not a game of "Rules." Bridge is a game of logic, judgment, and looking at the whole hand. With the hand above and no entry, it was correct to knock out the last trump before playing diamonds.

Of course, for the next six months, she will revert now to playing that 'extra' unnecessary round of trumps. Teaching bridge is a tough way to make a living.

I'm glad I don't have to. It's much easier being a radiologist.

DEAL 98   LET'S GET STARTED

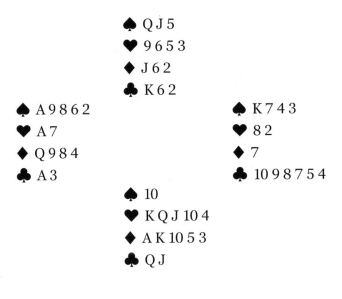

```
                     ♠ Q J 5
                     ♥ 9 6 5 3
                     ♦ J 6 2
                     ♣ K 6 2
        ♠ A 9 8 6 2              ♠ K 7 4 3
        ♥ A 7                    ♥ 8 2
        ♦ Q 9 8 4                ♦ 7
        ♣ A 3                    ♣ 10 9 8 7 5 4
                     ♠ 10
                     ♥ K Q J 10 4
                     ♦ A K 10 5 3
                     ♣ Q J
```

South	West	North	East
1♥	1♠	2♥	3♠
4♥		All Pass	

Opening Lead: ♦ 4

Declarer won the opening lead and without much thought, started the trumps by leading the king. West won the ace.

Still reluctant to lead a black suit with her aces, West led another diamond, East ruffed. Down one.

Was this avoidable? Unlucky? How could declarer have done better?

Maybe a little unlucky but declarer should have been concerned. In a situation like this, do you want the defender to win or duck the first round of trumps?

Duck, of course. So don't lead the king. Maybe try low towards the nine or lead the jack. Anything to try to sneak a round past West.

DEAL 99 BETTER TIMING

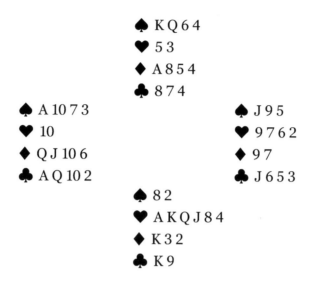

♠ K Q 6 4
♥ 5 3
♦ A 8 5 4
♣ 8 7 4

♠ A 10 7 3
♥ 10
♦ Q J 10 6
♣ A Q 10 2

♠ J 9 5
♥ 9 7 6 2
♦ 9 7
♣ J 6 5 3

♠ 8 2
♥ A K Q J 8 4
♦ K 3 2
♣ K 9

South	West	North	East
1 ♥	Dbl	1 NT	P
3 ♥	P	4 ♥	All Pass

Opening Lead: **♦** Queen

Declarer was looking at possibly one spade, two clubs, and one slow diamond loser. He won the diamond king, drew trumps and led a spade.

West ducked, the king winning. He tried returning to his hand with the club king, but West won the ace and continued diamonds. The four losers came true.

How should declarer have timed the hand?

Some hands go down for failing to draw trumps, others for drawing them too soon. The trump suit here was declarer's only means of transportation to his hand to lead spades.

Win the opening lead in hand and play a spade. If West ducks, South can play a heart now and lead another spade. The diamond ace will be an entry later to the good spade to discard a loser.

DEAL 100 DO YOU BELIEVE?

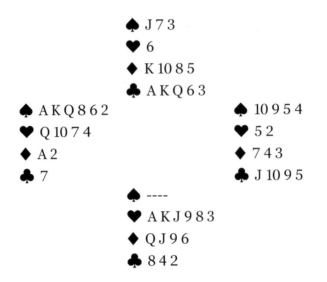

```
                    ♠ J 7 3
                    ♥ 6
                    ♦ K 10 8 5
                    ♣ A K Q 6 3
        ♠ A K Q 8 6 2              ♠ 10 9 5 4
        ♥ Q 10 7 4                 ♥ 5 2
        ♦ A 2                      ♦ 7 4 3
        ♣ 7                        ♣ J 10 9 5
                    ♠ ----
                    ♥ A K J 9 8 3
                    ♦ Q J 9 6
                    ♣ 8 4 2
```

North	East	South	West
1♣	P	1♥	1♠
P	3♠	4♥	Dbl
All Pass			

Opening Lead: ♠ Ace

Declarer ruffed the opening lead. He played the A-K of trumps and optimistically led a third trump, thinking maybe West had doubled on her good looks.

West cashed two high trumps and led another spade, forcing out declarers last trump. When the clubs didn't run, declarer had to touch the diamonds.
Down three.

Where did declarer go wrong? How would you have played?

Whether or not you believe West, declarer can assure the contract after two rounds of trumps by starting on diamonds. What can the defense do?

West can force declarer but South now is ahead in the race. He can ruff the spade return and cash his minor suit winners, losing only two trumps and one diamond.

DEAL 101   WHAT'S THE PROBLEM?

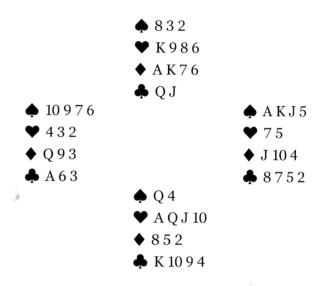

Contract: 4 ♥

Opening Lead: ♠ 10

Declarer ruffed the third round of spades and counted his tricks. Ten easy tricks. Four hearts, three clubs, two diamonds, and a spade ruff in hand. What could go wrong? He was about to find out.

South drew trumps. They were 3/2, no problem. OK, time to start on the clubs. He played the club queen which won. When he played the club jack, West won and played a diamond.

South is still in the dummy as you are reading this, trying to figure how to reach his good clubs to discard diamond losers.

Draw trumps, don't draw trumps, what's the right answer?

Somewhere in the middle. South can play two rounds of trumps, but he has to save the last round as the entry to the clubs. Two rounds of hearts, then one or two rounds of clubs, and back to his hand drawing the last trump in the process.

Yes, ten easy tricks. What was the problem?

DEAL 102   TRANSPORTATION

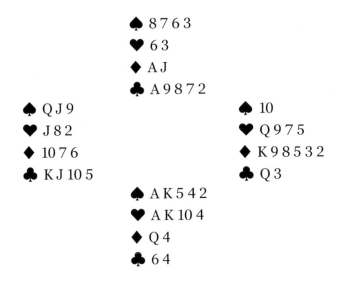

♠ 8 7 6 3
♥ 6 3
♦ A J
♣ A 9 8 7 2

♠ Q J 9
♥ J 8 2
♦ 10 7 6
♣ K J 10 5

♠ 10
♥ Q 9 7 5
♦ K 9 8 5 3 2
♣ Q 3

♠ A K 5 4 2
♥ A K 10 4
♦ Q 4
♣ 6 4

Contract: 4 ♠
Opening Lead: ♦ 6

Declarer played low, East won the king and returned a low heart. Declarer's plan was to ruff two hearts in dummy, easy if trumps are 2/2.

But there may be transportation problems. Declarer cashed the A-K of trumps. He cashed the other high heart and ruffed a heart.

Now the light went off. How do I get back to my hand? He played ace and a club. West won and cashed another round of trumps. No more heart ruffs.

Down one.

How could declarer have arranged for a second heart ruff?

Two ways actually. After one round of trumps, play ace and a low club. Win the return and play the second high spade. If trumps are 2/2, he makes five.

If trumps are 3/1, ruff a club back to your hand. If you are overruffed, it's a trick they were getting anyhow.

Or win that heart shift and play one trump. Then ruff a heart and come back with a trump. Now you can ruff another heart.

Anything but what the original declarer did.

DEAL 103   ROSY GLASSES

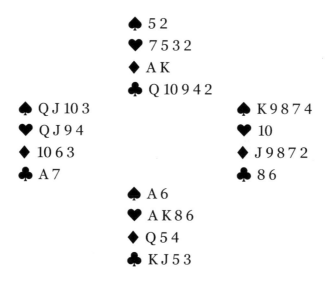

♠ 5 2
♥ 7 5 3 2
♦ A K
♣ Q 10 9 4 2

♠ Q J 10 3
♥ Q J 9 4
♦ 10 6 3
♣ A 7

♠ K 9 8 7 4
♥ 10
♦ J 9 8 7 2
♣ 8 6

♠ A 6
♥ A K 8 6
♦ Q 5 4
♣ K J 5 3

Contract: 4 ♥

Opening Lead: ♠ Queen

Declarer pictured three losers; one spade, one heart, and one club. Maybe the small spade could be discarded on the queen of diamonds. Then ruff the spade loser and make five? High hopes, things looked rosy.

So declarer won the spade ace and cashed the A-K of diamonds. Then a trump to the ace and the diamond queen, discarding the spade. He played another high trump, East showing out. He ruffed his spade loser, but when he led a club, West won, drew the trumps and cashed the spades for down three.

Whew, where were those rosy glasses now?

What was the better line of play?

The usual adage of side suits first. Force out the club ace while you still have trump control. Worst case scenario, the defense could get a club ruff, but declarer can keep control losing one club and two trumps.

And now put on the rosy glasses!

DEAL 104   HAND RECOGNITION

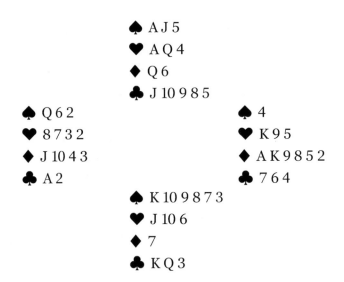

♠ A J 5
♥ A Q 4
♦ Q 6
♣ J 10 9 8 5

♠ Q 6 2
♥ 8 7 3 2
♦ J 10 4 3
♣ A 2

♠ 4
♥ K 9 5
♦ A K 9 8 5 2
♣ 7 6 4

♠ K 10 9 8 7 3
♥ J 10 6
♦ 7
♣ K Q 3

North	East	South	West
1♣	1♦	1♠	2♦
Dbl	P	4♠	All Pass

Opening Lead: ♦ Jack

Declarer started poorly by ducking the opening lead. East followed with the ♦2 so West shifted to a heart. East won the ♥K and played another high diamond which South ruffed.

South cashed the ♠AK, down one, still having to lose the ♣A.

How would you have played four spades for eleven tricks?

For starters, West is the danger hand. Declarer does not want a heart shift so he should play the ♦Q at Trick 1, not to win, but to transfer the lead. East doesn't have mirrors; he will almost surely play another high diamond which declarer ruffs.

Now, instead of relying on nursery rhymes, he can lead the ten of trumps and let it ride into East, the safe hand. Even if it loses, declarer has time to draw the rest of the trumps and set up the clubs to discard all his heart losers.

DEAL 105   OUT OF CONTROL

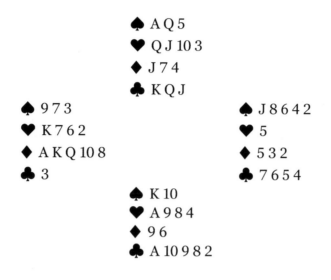

```
              ♠ A Q 5
              ♥ Q J 10 3
              ♦ J 7 4
              ♣ K Q J
  ♠ 9 7 3                    ♠ J 8 6 4 2
  ♥ K 7 6 2                  ♥ 5
  ♦ A K Q 10 8               ♦ 5 3 2
  ♣ 3                        ♣ 7 6 5 4
              ♠ K 10
              ♥ A 9 8 4
              ♦ 9 6
              ♣ A 10 9 8 2
```

West	North	East	South
1♦	Dbl	P	2♦
P	2♥	P	4♥
All Pass			

Opening Lead: ♦ Ace

Declarer ruffed the third round of diamonds. Since it was clear from the bidding West likely had the trump king, declarer started trumps by playing the ace and another. When West played low, South had no good continuation.

If he played a third trump, West would win and force dummy to ruff a diamond. Declarer had lost control and the contract.

How should you play to make four hearts?

The object is to force West to take his high trump and leave you to go about your business. Start with a low trump. If West ducks, offer him another. By keeping trumps in both hands, declarer remains in control.

This type of play is often useful holding something like A Q J 10 or A K J 10 opposite four small.

117

DEAL 106   READY OR NOT

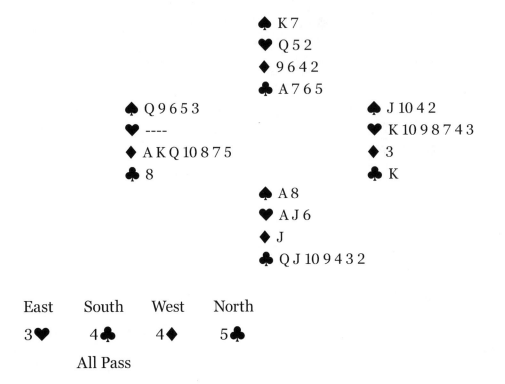

♠ K 7
♥ Q 5 2
♦ 9 6 4 2
♣ A 7 6 5

♠ Q 9 6 5 3
♥ ----
♦ A K Q 10 8 7 5
♣ 8

♠ J 10 4 2
♥ K 10 9 8 7 4 3
♦ 3
♣ K

♠ A 8
♥ A J 6
♦ J
♣ Q J 10 9 4 3 2

East	South	West	North
3♥	4♣	4♦	5♣
	All Pass		

Opening Lead: ♦ Ace

West led the A-K of diamonds. East discarded on the second diamond as declarer ruffed. With a likely heart loser, declarer led the club queen, West played the eight.

Declarer had to guess and played low. East won and played a spade.

Declarer still had a late heart loser. Down one.

What should declarer have played at Trick 3?

Declarer need see that there was a bit of work to do first. Cash the A-K of spades before touching the trumps. Now declarer can take the club finesse, not caring if it won or lost.

East won his singleton king, but he was endplayed. A heart return meant South had no heart losers, a spade return would give declarer a ruff/sluff.

DEAL 107   TRADE YA'

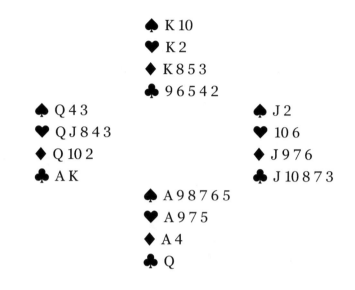

♠ K 10
♥ K 2
♦ K 8 5 3
♣ 9 6 5 4 2

♠ Q 4 3
♥ Q J 8 4 3
♦ Q 10 2
♣ A K

♠ J 2
♥ 10 6
♦ J 9 7 6
♣ J 10 8 7 3

♠ A 9 8 7 6 5
♥ A 9 7 5
♦ A 4
♣ Q

West	North	East	South
1♥	P	1NT	2♠
P	3♠	P	4♠
	All Pass		

Opening Lead: ♣ Ace

Declarer ruffed the second club. He played the A-K of hearts and ruffed a heart with dummy's spade ten. East overruffed with the jack and returned a trump.

When the trump queen did not fall, declarer was down one.

Was there a line of play that would combine several chances?

What a shock! East had only two hearts after West opened one heart. Ruff the first heart with dummy's spade king.

Now declarer can cross to his diamond ace and ruff his last heart with the spade ten. East can overruff but declarer is trading a heart loser while drawing trumps in an offbeat fashion.

Making four spades, losing two trump tricks and one club.

119

DEAL 108   DON'T MISTIME THIS ONE

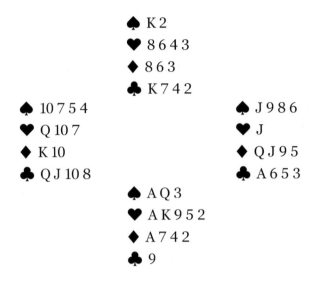

```
              ♠ K 2
              ♥ 8 6 4 3
              ♦ 8 6 3
              ♣ K 7 4 2
♠ 10 7 5 4                    ♠ J 9 8 6
♥ Q 10 7                      ♥ J
♦ K 10                        ♦ Q J 9 5
♣ Q J 10 8                    ♣ A 6 5 3
              ♠ A Q 3
              ♥ A K 9 5 2
              ♦ A 7 4 2
              ♣ 9
```

Contract: 4 ♥

Opening Lead: ♣ Queen

Declarer ruffed the second club, leaving the king in dummy. He played the A-K of trumps, planning to discard a diamond from dummy on the third spade, give up one diamond and ruff the rest. Easy game. When East showed out on the second trump, maybe not so easy?

When he gave up a diamond, West played another round of trumps, leaving only one in dummy. Declarer had an extra diamond loser. Down one.

Was this the right game plan? If so, how should declarer have played?

Right game plan, wrong timing. If trumps are 2/2, fine. After ruffing the club, play one top trump, then lead a low diamond, a trick you are going to lose anyhow.

West will win and continue clubs, but South ruffs and now can play the other high trump. When East shows out, South plays spades, discarding a diamond from dummy. South now can play ace of diamonds and can't be prevented from ruffing twice in dummy.

DEAL 109 ANOTHER SPEEDING TICKET

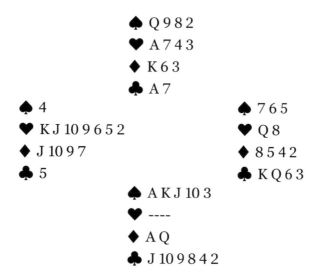

♠ Q 9 8 2
♥ A 7 4 3
♦ K 6 3
♣ A 7

♠ 4
♥ K J 10 9 6 5 2
♦ J 10 9 7
♣ 5

♠ 7 6 5
♥ Q 8
♦ 8 5 4 2
♣ K Q 6 3

♠ A K J 10 3
♥ ----
♦ A Q
♣ J 10 9 8 4 2

North	East	South	West
1♦	P	1♠	3♥
3♠	P	4♦	P
4♥	P	5♠	P
6♣	P	6♠	All Pass

Opening Lead: ♦ Jack

Declarer won the opening lead and drew trumps in three rounds. He played ace, then a low club. East won and returned another diamond.

Declarer won and ruffed a club in dummy, but still had another losing club. Down one.

How would you play to make the slam?

Declarer should have received a speeding ticket. He was in too much of a hurry to draw trumps. He needed to ruff some clubs first.

After winning the opening lead, start the clubs; ace and another. Now he will have time, even with a trump return, to ruff clubs twice before drawing trumps.
The remaining clubs are high.

DEAL 110   GETTING READY

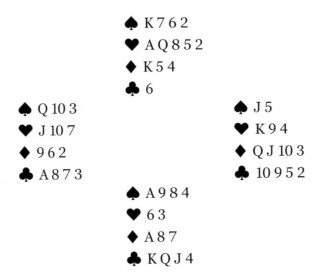

♠ K 7 6 2
♥ A Q 8 5 2
♦ K 5 4
♣ 6

♠ Q 10 3
♥ J 10 7
♦ 9 6 2
♣ A 8 7 3

♠ J 5
♥ K 9 4
♦ Q J 10 3
♣ 10 9 5 2

♠ A 9 8 4
♥ 6 3
♦ A 8 7
♣ K Q J 4

Contract: 4 ♠

Opening Lead: ♦ 2

Declarer won the ♦K, cashed the ♠AK and led a club to his king. West won, cashed the last trump and led a diamond. Declarer won the ♦A, cashed a high club discarding a diamond from dummy and took a losing heart finesse.

East returned a diamond, ruffed with dummy's last trump. Declarer cashed the ♥A and ruffed a low heart. But he still had a losing club.

Down one, losing one spade, one heart, and two clubs.

Wrong game plan? Wrong timing? Wrong what?

Not a bad game plan, but wrong timing. What kind of hand is this? Sort of a crossruff? So it's often a bad idea to draw trumps when there is other work to be done. The key is not letting the defender play that third round of trumps.

Win the diamond king and force out the club ace. Win the diamond return and discard the diamond loser. Take the losing heart finesse.

Now you are ready for your crossruff. Cash two high trumps and go about your business, losing only one more trick in the end to the high trump.

DEAL 111   FIGHTING FUTILITY

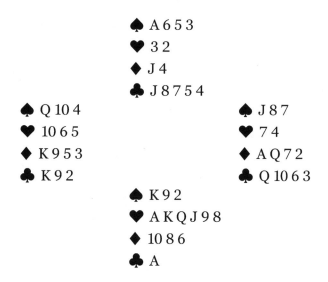

```
              ♠ A 6 5 3
              ♥ 3 2
              ♦ J 4
              ♣ J 8 7 5 4
♠ Q 10 4                      ♠ J 8 7
♥ 10 6 5                      ♥ 7 4
♦ K 9 5 3                     ♦ A Q 7 2
♣ K 9 2                       ♣ Q 10 6 3
              ♠ K 9 2
              ♥ A K Q J 9 8
              ♦ 10 8 6
              ♣ A
```

Contract: 4 ♥

Opening Lead: ♦ 3

Starting with nine tricks, declarer's plan was to ruff a diamond for his tenth trick. East won the opening lead and returned a trump. Hoping maybe at least one opponent was brain dead, declarer led another diamond.

But the defender who won this trick was not yet on life support and returned a trump. Declarer finished with the nine tricks he started with. Down one.

Where do you find the tenth trick?

Declarer should see the futility of trying for a diamond ruff. Instead, play a low spade from both hands at Trick 3, while there is a trump in dummy.

When spades are 3/3, declarer had ten tricks.

DEAL 112   FOCUS ON THE HAND

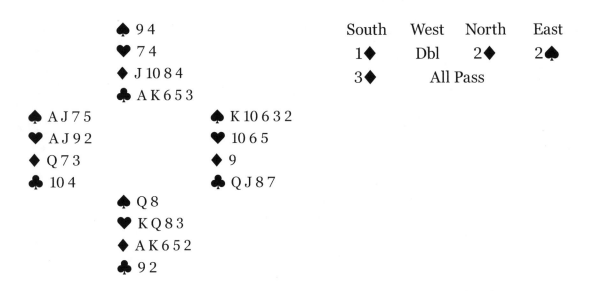

♠ 9 4
♥ 7 4
♦ J 10 8 4
♣ A K 6 5 3

♠ A J 7 5
♥ A J 9 2
♦ Q 7 3
♣ 10 4

♠ K 10 6 3 2
♥ 10 6 5
♦ 9
♣ Q J 8 7

♠ Q 8
♥ K Q 8 3
♦ A K 6 5 2
♣ 9 2

South	West	North	East
1♦	Dbl	2♦	2♠
3♦	All Pass		

Opening Lead: ♣ 10

Maybe E/W should have competed to three spades. Declarer won the ♣A and cashed the ♦AK, (saying something about getting the kiddies off the street). He then led a club to the king and ruffed a club, hoping for a 3/3 split.

Declarer led the ♥K. West won and made the good play defenders often fail to find. He cashed the high trump, the ♦Q This left declarer with too many losers: Two spades, two hearts and one diamond.

How would you have handled the trump suit?

Remember it's a bridge hand, not just a trump suit. South should play a heart at Trick 2 to his king. No matter what, he would be able to ruff two hearts in dummy.

DEAL 113   THE CAR WON'T START

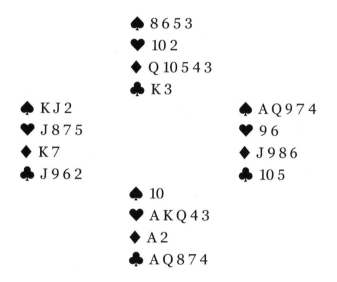

♠ 8 6 5 3
♥ 10 2
♦ Q 10 5 4 3
♣ K 3

♠ K J 2
♥ J 8 7 5
♦ K 7
♣ J 9 6 2

♠ A Q 9 7 4
♥ 9 6
♦ J 9 8 6
♣ 10 5

♠ 10
♥ A K Q 4 3
♦ A 2
♣ A Q 8 7 4

Contract: 4 ♥

Opening Lead: ♠ 2

East won the opening lead and returned a trump. Declarer, seeing no problems and lots of tricks, cashed the ♥AKQ. He lost a trick in each suit, down one. At least he got it over quickly. Sure, swift, and wrong.

How would a more cautious declarer have played?

What can go wrong? Everything, of course. The trumps will be 4/1, the clubs 4/2, the car won't start, just a bad day all around.

Win the trump at Trick 2 and play three rounds of clubs. If they are 3/3, great! If 4/2, West may have the ♥J in which case the ♥10 will win. Or West may have four hearts and four clubs.

In this case, you ruff the club, the ♥10 wins. Now cross to the ♦A, play the top hearts and then just keep the clubs coming.

You lose one spade, one diamond, and one heart.

DEAL 114 'RESERVE' TRUMPS

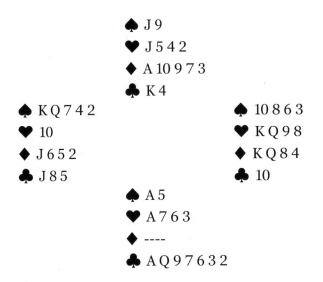

♠ J 9
♥ J 5 4 2
♦ A 10 9 7 3
♣ K 4

♠ K Q 7 4 2
♥ 10
♦ J 6 5 2
♣ J 8 5

♠ 10 8 6 3
♥ K Q 9 8
♦ K Q 8 4
♣ 10

♠ A 5
♥ A 7 6 3
♦ ----
♣ A Q 9 7 6 3 2

South	North
1♣	1♦
1♥	2♥
3♣	4♥
P	

Opening Lead: ♠ King

Declarer won the ♠A and crossed to dummy's ♣K. He discarded his spade loser on the ♦A. He played a heart to his ♥A and led a low heart.

Ouch! West drew trumps and took the rest of the tricks.

How would you have kept control?

Everything was fine until Trick 4. When it was clear that the club suit was good and hearts no worse than 4-1, declarer should draw trumps using what the great Swedish player Jan Wohlin called 'reserve trumps', the clubs.

Declarer can afford to lose three trump tricks, so just keep playing clubs.

Now it's back and forth. East can ruff and return anything. South ruffs, more clubs, more ruffs, etc, etc, etc. The defense scores three trump tricks, but declarer remains in control.

Declarer is drawing trumps with the clubs, the reserve trumps.

DEAL 115   YOU LOST WHAT?

                          ♠ K J 4
                          ♥ K 6 4
                          ♦ K
                          ♣ J 9 7 6 5 2
        ♠ 9   ♠ 10 8 7 6
        ♥ J 10 7   ♥ A Q 9 5 3 2
        ♦ J 9 7 3   ♦ 10
        ♣ K 10 8 4 3   ♣ A Q
                          ♠ A Q 5 3 2
                          ♥ 8
                          ♦ A Q 8 6 5 4 2
                          ♣ void

South	West	North	East
1♦	P	2♣	2♥
2♠	P	2NT	P
3♠	P	4♠	All Pass

Opening Lead: ♥ Jack

Declarer ruffed the second heart. He played a low spade to the ♠K, then the ♠J, and West discarded. Declarer unblocked the ♦K and led to the ♠A. After drawing the last trump with his last trump, he continued the diamonds. But since diamonds were 4/1, he lost control. Down two.

How could declarer keep control and make his contract?

When in danger of being shortened, think of the principles of side suits first and reserve trumps. After ruffing the second heart, play a diamond to the ♦K and a trump to your ♠A. Since nothing is breaking worse than 4/1, you are OK.

Ruff a low diamond with the ♠K. Now the ♠J to the ♠Q. This may seem strange, creating an extra trump trick for the defense, but you have no other safe means back to your long diamonds.

Now put your reserve trumps to work. Just keep those diamonds coming. You have lost only one trick and can afford to lose two more trump tricks.

DEAL 116   BEEN THERE

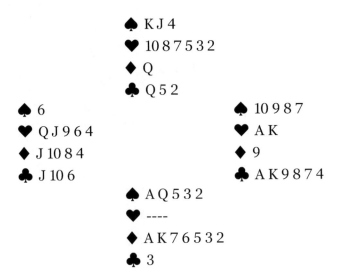

```
                    ♠ K J 4
                    ♥ 10 8 7 5 3 2
                    ♦ Q
                    ♣ Q 5 2
        ♠ 6                         ♠ 10 9 8 7
        ♥ Q J 9 6 4                 ♥ A K
        ♦ J 10 8 4                  ♦ 9
        ♣ J 10 6                    ♣ A K 9 8 7 4
                    ♠ A Q 5 3 2
                    ♥ ----
                    ♦ A K 7 6 5 3 2
                    ♣ 3
```

South	West	North	East
1♦	P	1♥	2♣
2♠	P	3♥	P
3♠	P	4♠	Dbl
	All Pass		

Opening Lead: ♥ Jack

East's double was probably not best. South ruffed the second club. Anticipating bad breaks, he led a diamond to the queen. He played a trump to his ace and ruffed a diamond with dummy's king of trumps.

Then declarer played the trump jack to his queen, again sacrificing a trump trick, but maintaining control.

Now declarer just kept those diamonds coming, losing only two trump tricks and one club. Making four spades, doubled.

Thanks for Frank Stewart for this example of the theme we have been discussing, reserve trumps.

DEAL 117   FORGET ABOUT IT

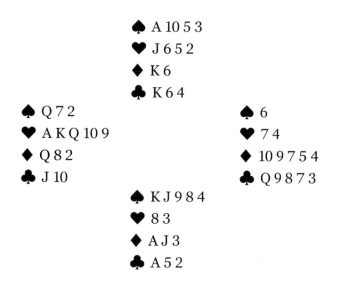

- ♠ A 10 5 3
- ♥ J 6 5 2
- ♦ K 6
- ♣ K 6 4

- ♠ Q 7 2
- ♥ A K Q 10 9
- ♦ Q 8 2
- ♣ J 10

- ♠ 6
- ♥ 7 4
- ♦ 10 9 7 5 4
- ♣ Q 9 8 7 3

- ♠ K J 9 8 4
- ♥ 8 3
- ♦ A J 3
- ♣ A 5 2

South	West	North	East
1♠	2♥	3♥	P
4♠	All Pass		

Opening Lead: ♥ Ace

West cashed the ♥AK and shifted to the ♣J. South won and cashed the ♠AK. Then declarer cashed the ♦K and took a diamond finesse, hoping to get rid of the club loser.

Unlucky, down one.

How should declarer have handled the trump suit?

By keeping his fingers off the trumps altogether. Cash the ♣AK, ruff a heart, cash the ♦AK, ruff the ♦J and ruff the last heart.

At Trick 10 declarer exits with a club. Dummy has ♠A105 and South has ♠KJ9. The defenders are on lead so South takes the last three trump tricks.

DEAL 118   NO PROBLEM

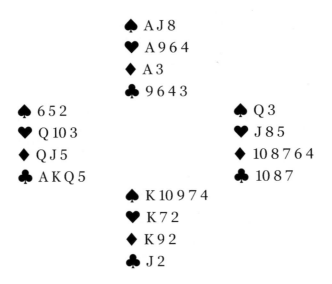

```
              ♠ A J 8
              ♥ A 9 6 4
              ♦ A 3
              ♣ 9 6 4 3
♠ 6 5 2                    ♠ Q 3
♥ Q 10 3                   ♥ J 8 5
♦ Q J 5                    ♦ 10 8 7 6 4
♣ A K Q 5                  ♣ 10 8 7
              ♠ K 10 9 7 4
              ♥ K 7 2
              ♦ K 9 2
              ♣ J 2
```

West	North	East	South
1♣	P	P	1♠
P	4♠	All Pass	

Opening Leader: ♣ Ace

Declarer ruffed the third club and played West for the spade queen. South also had a slow heart loser, down one.

What was the right way to play the trumps? Why?

This is another example of just keeping your fingers off the trumps. After ruffing the third club, cash the ♥AK, the ♦AK and ruffed a diamond in dummy.

After ruffing dummy's last club, exit with a heart.

Dummy now has the ♠AJ and a heart, declarer the ♠K109. With a defender on lead, declarer also has the rest of the tricks.

Making four spades.

DEAL 119   MR. SMILEY

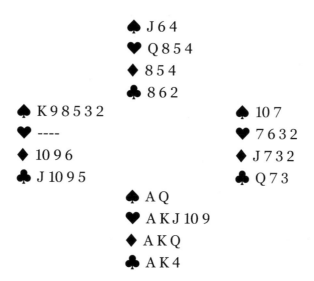

♠ J 6 4
♥ Q 8 5 4
♦ 8 5 4
♣ 8 6 2

♠ K 9 8 5 3 2
♥ ----
♦ 10 9 6
♣ J 10 9 5

♠ 10 7
♥ 7 6 3 2
♦ J 7 3 2
♣ Q 7 3

♠ A Q
♥ A K J 10 9
♦ A K Q
♣ A K 4

Contract: 6 ♥
Opening Lead: ♣ Jack

Declarer won the opening lead and foreseeing no problem, started to draw trumps. His plan was to discard the club loser on the jack of spades. He drew three rounds of trumps, then played the ace and queen of spades.

West won and played another spade. East ruffed. Down one.

What was the proper timing of the trumps?

After one round of trumps, there is the potential danger of playing more trumps. Played the queen of spades before any more trumps. West has to win.

Win the club return, unblocked the spade ace and finished the trumps in dummy where the spade jack is waiting with a smile 🙂.

Making six hearts.

DEAL 120 BETTER TIMING

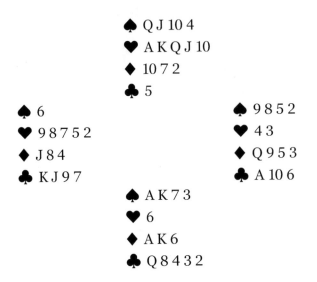

♠ Q J 10 4
♥ A K Q J 10
♦ 10 7 2
♣ 5

♠ 6
♥ 9 8 7 5 2
♦ J 8 4
♣ K J 9 7

♠ 9 8 5 2
♥ 4 3
♦ Q 9 5 3
♣ A 10 6

♠ A K 7 3
♥ 6
♦ A K 6
♣ Q 8 4 3 2

Contract: 6 ♠

Opening Lead: ♥ 9

Declarer counted eleven top tricks plus a ruff. He won the opening lead and played the trump ace and a trump to dummy. When West showed out, declarer led a club. East won and returned a trump.

Declarer continued hearts, East ruffing the third round. Declarer overruffed, but still had a diamond loser at the end.

Down one.

Can declarer overcome the bad trump split?

Declarer can lead a trump to the ace at Trick 2. But then cash the A-K of diamonds before leading a second trump. Discard a diamond on a high heart and ruffed the last diamond with the spade king.

Now draw trumps and you have your twelve tricks.

DEAL 121 FIRST THINGS FIRST

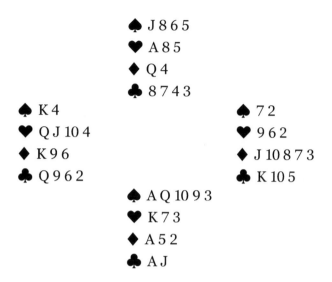

```
                    ♠ J 8 6 5
                    ♥ A 8 5
                    ♦ Q 4
                    ♣ 8 7 4 3
   ♠ K 4                        ♠ 7 2
   ♥ Q J 10 4                   ♥ 9 6 2
   ♦ K 9 6                      ♦ J 10 8 7 3
   ♣ Q 9 6 2                    ♣ K 10 5
                    ♠ A Q 10 9 3
                    ♥ K 7 3
                    ♦ A 5 2
                    ♣ A J
```

Contract: 4 ♠

Opening Lead: ♥ Queen

Declarer won the opening lead in dummy to take a trump finesse. West won and played another heart.

Declarer won, but now with a loser in every suit, went down one.

Could declarer have timed this better?

As my friend Frank Stewart says, "First things first, but not necessarily in that order."

Declarer can avoid a heart loser by trying a diamond finesse first to discard the heart loser.

Win the opening lead in hand and lead a diamond. West wins and plays another heart. South wins in dummy, cashes the diamond queen and can cross to his hand with the club ace to discard the heart loser on the ace of diamonds.

DEAL 122   WATCH YOUR STEP

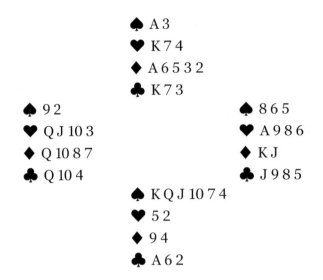

♠ A 3
♥ K 7 4
♦ A 6 5 3 2
♣ K 7 3

♠ 9 2
♥ Q J 10 3
♦ Q 10 8 7
♣ Q 10 4

♠ 8 6 5
♥ A 9 8 6
♦ K J
♣ J 9 8 5

♠ K Q J 10 7 4
♥ 5 2
♦ 9 4
♣ A 6 2

Contract: 4 ♠
Opening Lead: ♥ Queen

Declarer ruffed the third heart and drew trumps. Then he led a low diamond from both hands. East won and played another heart.

Declarer ruffed, cashed the ace of diamonds and ruffed a diamond. When East discarded, South still had a club loser.

Was South in too much of a hurry to draw trumps?

Yes. Trick 4 is the time to concede a diamond. Declarer needs all the entries he can find to help set up the diamonds. If East now leads a trump, declarer wins in hand and continues diamonds.

The trump ace provides the extra entry to set up and use the last diamond to discard the club.

DEAL 123 MISSED THE LAST BUS HOME

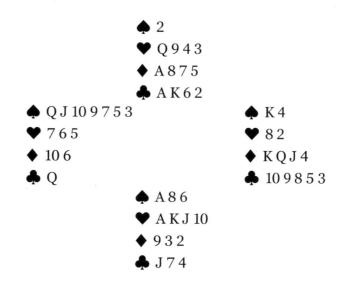

♠ 2
♥ Q 9 4 3
♦ A 8 7 5
♣ A K 6 2

♠ Q J 10 9 7 5 3
♥ 7 6 5
♦ 10 6
♣ Q

♠ K 4
♥ 8 2
♦ K Q J 4
♣ 10 9 8 5 3

♠ A 8 6
♥ A K J 10
♦ 9 3 2
♣ J 7 4

South	West	North	East
1♣	2♠	Dbl	P
3♥	P	4♥	All Pass

Opening Lead: ♠ Queen

Declarer won the opening lead and cashed the ♥A. Needing to trump spades, she ruffed one spade low, played a heart to her hand and ruffed her last spade high. So far so good but now how could she get back to draw the last trump?

Declarer led a low club. West won the queen and played a diamond. Declarer could not prevent East getting in to give West a club ruff. Down one.

Declarer might have guessed to cash the club ace and lead another club. If West doesn't have the last trump she will be fine. If he does ruff the club jack at least declarer will make her contract.

Could declarer have avoided this whole problem?

At Trick 2, declarer should ruff a spade with the trump queen and came back to her hand with a trump. Ruff her last spade with the nine of hearts. Now there is a trump in dummy to return to her hand.

When the club queen falls, eleven easy tricks.

DEAL 124   JUST DO IT

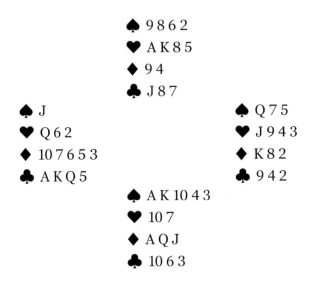

```
              ♠ 9 8 6 2
              ♥ A K 8 5
              ♦ 9 4
              ♣ J 8 7
♠ J                          ♠ Q 7 5
♥ Q 6 2                      ♥ J 9 4 3
♦ 10 7 6 5 3                 ♦ K 8 2
♣ A K Q 5                    ♣ 9 4 2
              ♠ A K 10 4 3
              ♥ 10 7
              ♦ A Q J
              ♣ 10 6 3
```

Contract: 2 ♠

Opening Lead: ♣ Ace

West cashes three top clubs and switches to a diamond. East plays the king and declarer wins the ace. When declarer cashes the spade ace, West plays the jack.

Should declarer play the spade king next or take a finesse? Nine never?

The finesse is a big favorite. Why? The theory of "Restricted Choice" is one of those topics you don't have to understand, you just do it.

When you led the ace, you saw the jack. You may think West is just as likely to have the jack and the queen, but that's not true.

Restricted choice says missing two equal honors, if you lead the ace and an opponent plays either one, it's likely he does not have the other.

For a full discussion, read the "Encyclopedia of Bridge." This is one of those facts of life you don't have to understand, you just do it.

The finesse is your best play.

A LOT OF THIS,

A LOT OF THAT

PARTNER, PLEASE, BETTER TRUMPS NEXT TIME

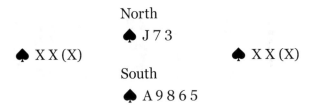

North
♠ J 7 3

♠ X X (X)   ♠ X X (X)

South
♠ A 9 8 6 5

You bid to six spades, these are your trumps and you have no losers in the other three suits no matter how badly you play. How will you handle the spades?

Assume the outstanding trumps are 3-2. What are our options? If East/West are:

WEST	EAST	
K10	Q42	Lead low towards the jack. If West takes the king, later lead the jack. If West plays the ten, later lead the ace to drop the king.
Q10	K42	Lead low towards the jack. If West takes the queen, later lead the jack. If West plays the ten, later lead the ace to drop the queen.
104	KQ2	Lead to the seven, losing to an honor. Later lead the jack.
KQ or 1042	1042 KQ	Lead ace and another, which drops one honor, then the other.
10	KQ42	Lead towards the jack & honor. Then the seven to finesse the other honor.

Be aware you have to do a lot of good guessing. The answers may be there if you can judge which combination to play for. In the meantime, find a partner who puts down more and better trumps.

DRAW TRUMPS: START HIGH OR LOW?

♠
♥ 2
♦
♣

♠
♥ K Q J 10 9 8
♦
♣

Contract: Some number of hearts

You are going to draw trumps. Which should you lead first?
High, low, middle, or it doesn't matter?

Everything in bridge matters. It depends on what you need and what you are trying to accomplish. Do you want to pull the trumps quickly or do you prefer to get a round or two thru before they take their ace?

If you want to pull them quickly, start with the king. And if they win the first or second round, finish drawing trumps from the top.

If you have a reason to sneak a round or two past the defenders, lead the eight. This will not tell the opponents about the quality of your suit. They might make a bad defensive decision, thinking their partner may have a trump trick.

Starting at the top, the opponents will know your suit is solid. I often see players do just the opposite; lead the eight with a smug look on their face, "Look how good my suit is, opponents," just in case they were wondering. Great!

DEAL 125   EQUAL?

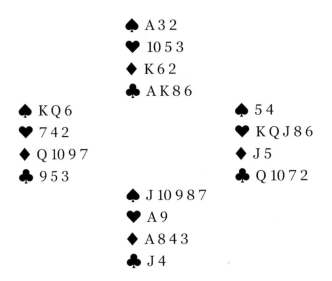

```
                    ♠ A 3 2
                    ♥ 10 5 3
                    ♦ K 6 2
                    ♣ A K 8 6
        ♠ K Q 6                  ♠ 5 4
        ♥ 7 4 2                  ♥ K Q J 8 6
        ♦ Q 10 9 7               ♦ J 5
        ♣ 9 5 3                  ♣ Q 10 7 2
                    ♠ J 10 9 8 7
                    ♥ A 9
                    ♦ A 8 4 3
                    ♣ J 4
```

North	East	South	West
1♣	1♥	1♠	P
2♠	P	4♠	All Pass

Opening Lead: ♥ 2

Declarer won the second heart. Probably needing to ruff a diamond, he drew one round of trumps by leading the ♠J. West played the queen. Declarer won the ace and led another trump. West won and led a third heart.

Declarer ruffed and led a diamond, ducked to West who cashed his high trump. Declarer cashed the ♦AK, but when East discarded, he had a losing diamond left. Down one.

How could declarer manage a needed diamond ruff?

At the other table, the declarer started the trumps by leading the seven, the 'same' as the jack but different. Would you see the need to split as West? When the seven wins, declarer can duck one round of diamonds.

After ruffing the third round of hearts, declarer can cash the ♠A, the ♦AK and still has a trump in dummy to ruff the diamond. Worth a try.

Equal is not always equal. Special thanks to Frank Stewart for this one.

DEAL 126   ASSUMTIONS

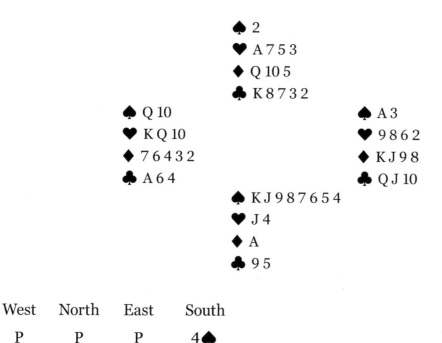

♠ 2
♥ A 7 5 3
♦ Q 10 5
♣ K 8 7 3 2

♠ Q 10
♥ K Q 10
♦ 7 6 4 3 2
♣ A 6 4

♠ A 3
♥ 9 8 6 2
♦ K J 9 8
♣ Q J 10

♠ K J 9 8 7 6 5 4
♥ J 4
♦ A
♣ 9 5

West	North	East	South
P	P	P	4♠

Opening Lead: ♥ King

To have any chance to make this contract, declarer saw he needed to hold his spade losers to one. He won the ♥A and played the ♠2. East played the three and declarer misguessed, playing the jack.

Down one. "Sorry," said South. "Were you in the men's room during the bidding?" asked North.

What was North referring to? What did South not hear?

Pass, Pass, Pass. You heard them, didn't you? So West has the ♥KQ. What's the club situation? Clubs, you ask? Why clubs?

Because to make four spades, declarer needs West to have the ♣A. So give it to him. Can he have the spade ace too? Seriously?

DEAL 127   PERCENTAGES OR WHAT?

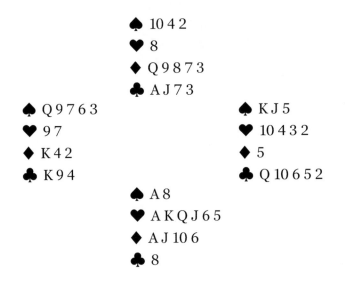

♠ 10 4 2
♥ 8
♦ Q 9 8 7 3
♣ A J 7 3

♠ Q 9 7 6 3
♥ 9 7
♦ K 4 2
♣ K 9 4

♠ K J 5
♥ 10 4 3 2
♦ 5
♣ Q 10 6 5 2

♠ A 8
♥ A K Q J 6 5
♦ A J 10 6
♣ 8

Contract: 6 ♦
Opening Lead: ♠ 6

The threatening opening lead presented South with many complex possibilities. A 50% diamond finesse? A 33% play on hearts, hoping they are 3/3 to discard two spades?

Declarer took the diamond finesse, down one.

Are there other ways to increase your chances?

Mike Lawrence pointed out another line of play to increase your chances. Cash the ♦A first, a 12% chance of dropping the ♦K. That failing, start the hearts discarding spades from dummy.

Here, for instance, if West ruffs the third heart low, overruff, ruff a club and do it again. If West ruffs with the diamond king, the spade loser still goes away.

Thanks, Mike.

DEAL 128   AT THE RACETRACK

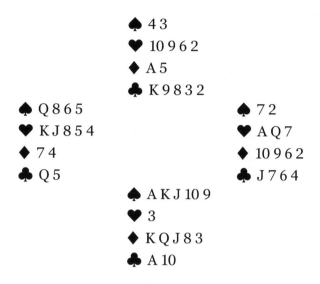

♠ 4 3
♥ 10 9 6 2
♦ A 5
♣ K 9 8 3 2

♠ Q 8 6 5   ♠ 7 2
♥ K J 8 5 4   ♥ A Q 7
♦ 7 4   ♦ 10 9 6 2
♣ Q 5   ♣ J 7 6 4

♠ A K J 10 9
♥ 3
♦ K Q J 8 3
♣ A 10

Contract: 4 ♠
Opening Lead: ♥ 5

Shortness in the long trump hand is a liability, not an asset. Declarer proved that here by ruffing the second heart and going to dummy's diamond ace. He took a spade finesse, back came another heart.

Declarer ruffed and cashed the A-K of trumps. When East discarded, declarer only had eight tricks. "Were you playing for overtricks?" asked North.

How should declarer take his ten tricks?

In danger of losing control with persistent heart plays, just cash the A-K of trumps and play on diamonds. The defense can ruff once with the eight and continue hearts, but declarer is ahead in the race for home.

Declarer keeps playing more diamonds, losing just one more trick to the trump queen. It's like the reserve trumps we discussed previously.

DEAL 129   YOU DID IT TO YOURSELF

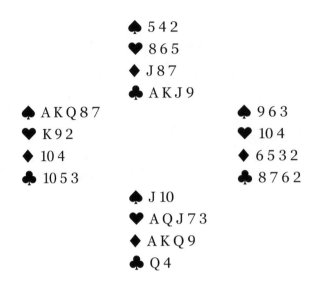

♠ 5 4 2
♥ 8 6 5
♦ J 8 7
♣ A K J 9

♠ A K Q 8 7
♥ K 9 2
♦ 10 4
♣ 10 5 3

♠ 9 6 3
♥ 10 4
♦ 6 5 3 2
♣ 8 7 6 2

♠ J 10
♥ A Q J 7 3
♦ A K Q 9
♣ Q 4

West	North	East	South
1♠	P	P	Dbl
P	2♣	P	2♥
P	3♥	P	4♥
All Pass			

Opening Lead: ♠ Ace

South ruffed the third round of spades. He went to dummy with a diamond and took a losing heart finesse. (What a surprise!) West led another spade.

East ruffed with the heart ten. South overruffed, but West now had another trump trick, the ♥92 behind declarers ♥A7. Down one.

Where was South during the bidding?

South set himself up for failure. The heart finesse was a waste of time and gave the defense a chance to do what it did. With only twelve missing high cards, who do you think has the ♥K?

Just start the trumps from the top and claim.

DEAL 130   WRONG DIRECTION

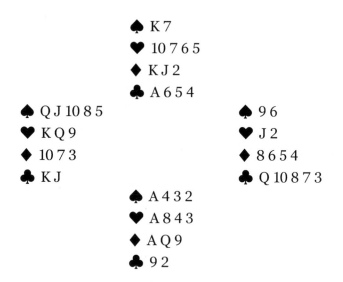

♠ K 7
♥ 10 7 6 5
♦ K J 2
♣ A 6 5 4

♠ Q J 10 8 5   ♠ 9 6
♥ K Q 9   ♥ J 2
♦ 10 7 3   ♦ 8 6 5 4
♣ K J   ♣ Q 10 8 7 3

♠ A 4 3 2
♥ A 8 4 3
♦ A Q 9
♣ 9 2

South	West	North	East
1♦	1♠	Dbl	P
2♥	P	3♥	P
4♥		All Pass	

Opening Lead: ♠ Queen

Declarer has a sure club loser and knew she needed trumps to be 3/2. Ruffing spades in dummy looked like a sensible line of play, but East rated to have only one or two spades. The possibility of an overruff loomed.

Declarer played ace and another trump. But West played a third round of trumps, leaving declarer one spade ruff short. Down one.

How should declarer have arranged two successful spade ruffs?

She played the hearts backwards. Win the spade king and play a low heart from each hand. Win the return, play the trump ace and now you can ruff two spades. You lose two trumps and one club.

145

DEAL 131   RIGHT IDEA BUT

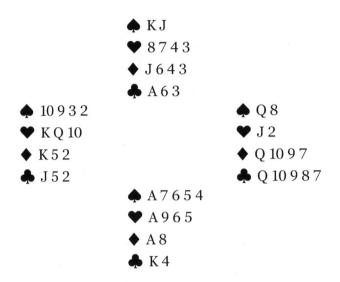

```
                    ♠ K J
                    ♥ 8 7 4 3
                    ♦ J 6 4 3
                    ♣ A 6 3
     ♠ 10 9 3 2                    ♠ Q 8
     ♥ K Q 10                      ♥ J 2
     ♦ K 5 2                       ♦ Q 10 9 7
     ♣ J 5 2                       ♣ Q 10 9 8 7
                    ♠ A 7 6 5 4
                    ♥ A 9 6 5
                    ♦ A 8
                    ♣ K 4
```

Contract: 4 ♥

Opening Lead: ♣ 2

South correctly saw this was a second suit hand. She won the opening lead and cashed the king, then ace of spades. But when she led a third spade and ruffed it, East overruffed with the jack.

She still had two trump losers and a diamond loser. Down one.

Poor game plan or what? You should have made four hearts.

Yes, the heart suit is far from robust, but this was a case of waiting too long to start drawing trumps. But she had to be careful how to do it. If you start with ace and another, the defenders may play a third round.

So just start low from both hands. West wins and plays another heart to your ace, East following. Now you can continue your plan to try to set up the spade suit.

You still have a heart and diamond to lose but you have ten tricks.

DEAL 132 HIGH LOW

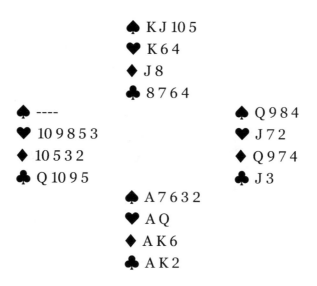

```
                    ♠ K J 10 5
                    ♥ K 6 4
                    ♦ J 8
                    ♣ 8 7 6 4
♠ ----                              ♠ Q 9 8 4
♥ 10 9 8 5 3                        ♥ J 7 2
♦ 10 5 3 2                          ♦ Q 9 7 4
♣ Q 10 9 5                          ♣ J 3
                    ♠ A 7 6 3 2
                    ♥ A Q
                    ♦ A K 6
                    ♣ A K 2
```

Contract: 6 ♠
Opening Lead: ♥ 10

Declarer was pleased with the contract; the club loser could go on the long heart, the low diamond could be ruffed and he could afford one trump loser.

He played the ♠A and could no longer make the contract. East now had one trick with the ♠Q and after declarer ruffed the diamond, East would score a second trump trick with the ♠9.

What is the proper line of play?

This is a good example of why bridge is a bridge hand, not just a suit.
At Trick 2, declarer should lead a low spade.

When West shows out, declarer can play the king or jack. But now he is going to be able to ruff his diamond with the spade five rather than an honor.

DEAL 133   WATCH CLOSELY

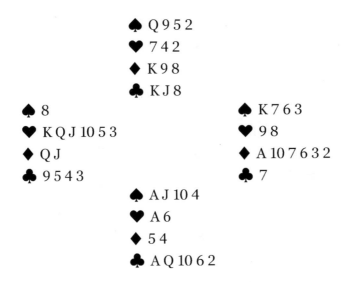

♠ Q 9 5 2
♥ 7 4 2
♦ K 9 8
♣ K J 8

♠ 8
♥ K Q J 10 5 3
♦ Q J
♣ 9 5 4 3

♠ K 7 6 3
♥ 9 8
♦ A 10 7 6 3 2
♣ 7

♠ A J 10 4
♥ A 6
♦ 5 4
♣ A Q 10 6 2

Contract: 4 ♠ (West overcalls 2 ♥)
Opening Lead: ♥ King

Declarer won the opening lead and crossed to dummy with a club. He led the spade queen. East played low, declarer played the four. Declarer repeated the finesse, now having to win in hand.

Now he was stuck there. If he played a club, East would ruff and play a heart to West. Now either the queen of diamonds thru dummy or another ruff will defeat the contract.

If declarer tries to get to dummy with a diamond East would win, same problem.

And the simple solution is?

If you start with the spade nine, then the queen, or unblock the first time under the queen, the lead remains in the dummy.

You end up with four spades, five clubs, and the heart ace.

That's ten, count'em, ten tricks for the good guys.

DEAL 134   SELF EXECUTION

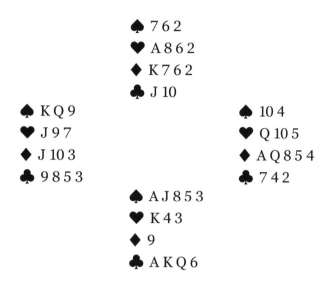

♠ 7 6 2
♥ A 8 6 2
♦ K 7 6 2
♣ J 10

♠ K Q 9
♥ J 9 7
♦ J 10 3
♣ 9 8 5 3

♠ 10 4
♥ Q 10 5
♦ A Q 8 5 4
♣ 7 4 2

♠ A J 8 5 3
♥ K 4 3
♦ 9
♣ A K Q 6

Contract: 4 ♠

Opening Lead: ♦ Jack

Declarer played low and ruffed the second diamond. He knew he needed trumps to be 3/2 and led ace and another, hoping he could later discard two of dummy's hearts on the good clubs and ruff a heart in dummy.

But West played a third trump and declarer ended losing two trump tricks, one heart and one diamond. Down one.

Right idea, wrong execution? Self execution? What would you do?

Right idea, wrong execution. Declarer has to ruff a heart. So if leading ace and another doesn't work, what might? How about starting with a low trump?

You will take the next trick and now lead the ace of trumps. After that, go about your business. Run clubs, discard a couple of hearts and you can't be prevented from ruffing a heart in dummy.

DEAL 135   TEN IMPS

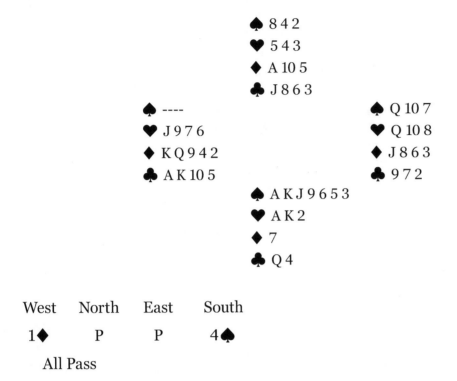

♠ 8 4 2
♥ 5 4 3
♦ A 10 5
♣ J 8 6 3

♠ ----
♥ J 9 7 6
♦ K Q 9 4 2
♣ A K 10 5

♠ Q 10 7
♥ Q 10 8
♦ J 8 6 3
♣ 9 7 2

♠ A K J 9 6 5 3
♥ A K 2
♦ 7
♣ Q 4

West	North	East	South
1♦	P	P	4♠
All Pass			

Opening Lead: ♣ Ace

In the last round of a Swiss team match, West switched to the diamond king. Declarer won the ace and played a spade to his ace. Down one.

How did he explain losing 10 IMP's to his teammates?

Declarer can assure his contract. Take the spade finesse. If it loses, force out the club king and discard your heart loser on the club jack. Use the spade eight as the entry.

If West has ♠Q107 there is nothing you can do. If spades are 2/1, you can't go down. Playing matchpoints, it's probably (?) right to cash the top spades, playing for the overtrick.

DEAL 136　NURSERY RHYMES

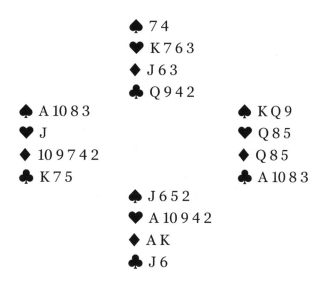

Contract:　2 ♥ (opponents could have/should have given you a push?)
Opening Lead:　♦ 10

Happy to be left in play at the two level, South won the opening lead and led a low heart, West played the jack, East the five. On the next trump from dummy, East played the eight, declarer went up ace (eight ever, nine never?), West showed out.

Declarer led a spade, East won, cashed the high trump, and played two more rounds of spades forcing out dummy's last trump. Declarer still had to lose two clubs and another spade. Down one.

Finesse or no finesse? Why? Restricted Choice? What's that?

100% to finesse, even if you never heard of Restricted Choice. If the finesse loses, declarer can ruff two spades in dummy. If it wins, he draws the last trump. Eight tricks: five trumps, two diamonds, and one spade ruff. A win-win situation.

The Rule of Restricted Choice: "which of two holdings a defender is more likely to have played from, assume he had no choice rather than he exercised a choice with equal cards."

Complicated but in other words, if he played the queen (or jack), assume he had no choice rather than he choose one from Q J.

DEAL 137   TAKE THE FREE GIFT

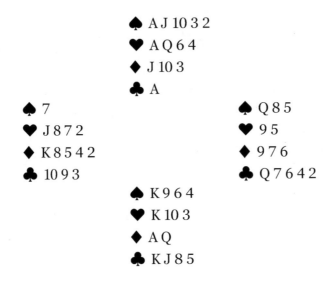

♠ A J 10 3 2
♥ A Q 6 4
♦ J 10 3
♣ A

♠ 7
♥ J 8 7 2
♦ K 8 5 4 2
♣ 10 9 3

♠ Q 8 5
♥ 9 5
♦ 9 7 6
♣ Q 7 6 4 2

♠ K 9 6 4
♥ K 10 3
♦ A Q
♣ K J 8 5

Contract: 6 ♠

Opening Lead: ♣ 10

Declarer won the opening lead and considered the trump suit. No clues, finesse either way or play for the drop with nine. He cashed the A-K, West showed out on the second round.

OK, not down yet. Declarer tried to ruff out the club queen or drop the heart jack but finally had to take the diamond finesse and of course West had the king.

"Really unlucky," lamented South. North muttered something under his breath about the hand being cold.

What line of play was North referring to?

A good example of considering the whole hand, not an isolated suit. After cashing the ace of trumps, declarer should let the jack of trump ride.

If the finesse loses, West is endplayed in three suits and South gets a free finesse somewhere. Making six spades.

DEAL 138   FINESSE OR DROP

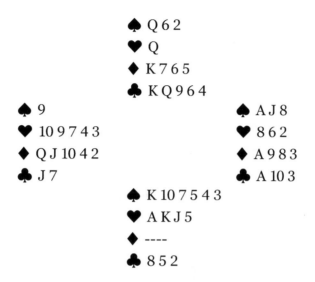

Contract: 4 ♠

Opening Lead: ♦ Queen

South ruffed the opening lead and played a trump to the queen. East won the ace and returned a trump. Declarer pondered for awhile (in a book it's almost always right to finesse) and played the king. West discarded.

South cashed the heart queen, ruffed a diamond and led a club. East won the ace and cashed the high trump. South still had one more club loser for down one.

Why, oh why? What ever happened to "Eight ever, nine never?"

Again, it's a bridge hand, not "spades". Even if the finesse loses, declarer can now discard three clubs on the high hearts and there is a trump in dummy to ruff the last club.

Declarer would lose only two spades and one club.

DEAL 139   DRAWING TRUMPS: FINESSE OR DROP

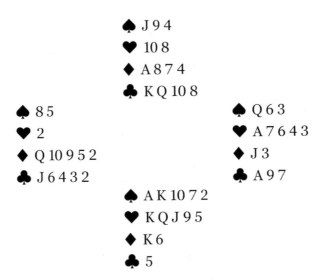

♠ J 9 4
♥ 10 8
♦ A 8 7 4
♣ K Q 10 8

♠ 8 5
♥ 2
♦ Q 10 9 5 2
♣ J 6 4 3 2

♠ Q 6 3
♥ A 7 6 4 3
♦ J 3
♣ A 9 7

♠ A K 10 7 2
♥ K Q J 9 5
♦ K 6
♣ 5

South	North
1♠	1NT
2♥	3♠
4♠	P

Opening Lead: ♥ 2

East wins the opening lead with the ace, cashes the club ace and returns a heart for West to ruff. West ruffs with the spade five and returns a diamond.

Declarer wins and cashes the ♠AK. West shows out on the second round. Down one.

"Are you paying any attention?" asked North.

What was North referring to? Did you notice the negative inference?

Why did East defend the way she did? If she didn't have the spade queen, she would try to give West two heart ruffs, hoping for a trump promotion.
Since the highest trump in dummy is the ♠J, maybe West had ♠ Q x.
But that defense would give away the location of the queen.

154

DEAL 140 VISIONS GO UP IN SMOKE

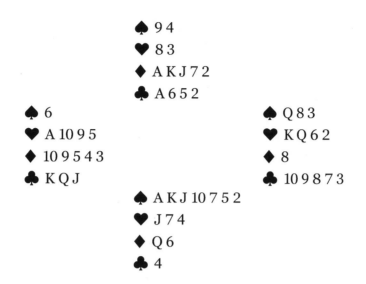

♠ 9 4
♥ 8 3
♦ A K J 7 2
♣ A 6 5 2

♠ 6
♥ A 10 9 5
♦ 10 9 5 4 3
♣ K Q J

♠ Q 8 3
♥ K Q 6 2
♦ 8
♣ 10 9 8 7 3

♠ A K J 10 7 5 2
♥ J 7 4
♦ Q 6
♣ 4

Contract: 4 ♠
Opening Lead: ♣ King

South won the opening lead and had visions of thirteen possible tricks if the spade queen fell. With nine trumps he cashed the A-K. But West (of course) discarded on the second spade.

Declarer tried to run the diamonds, but East ruffed the second diamond and cashed three heart tricks. Down one. So much for thirteen.

Could you have assured at least ten?

Usually with nine pieces it's right to play for the drop. But again, look at the hand. Forget thirteen. If you take a first round finesse and it loses, there is still a trump in dummy.

The defense would only take two hearts and one spade.

DEAL 141   EVEN THE CADDIE KNEW

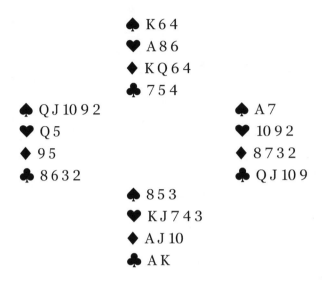

♠ K 6 4
♥ A 8 6
♦ K Q 6 4
♣ 7 5 4

♠ Q J 10 9 2
♥ Q 5
♦ 9 5
♣ 8 6 3 2

♠ A 7
♥ 10 9 2
♦ 8 7 3 2
♣ Q J 10 9

♠ 8 5 3
♥ K J 7 4 3
♦ A J 10
♣ A K

Contract: 4 ♥

Opening Lead: ♠ Queen

Since East surely has the spade ace, declarer played low. West continued with the jack, low, ace from East. East returned the club queen. Declarer won the ace, led a heart to the ace in dummy, both defenders following low, and led a heart from dummy.

East played the nine. Declarer thought, looked at the ceiling, and finessed. West won the queen and gave East a spade ruff.

Do you want South's phone number to schedule a game?

This is just an example of being a slave to sayings like "Eight ever, nine never."

Playing the king ensures ten tricks. Heck, my caddie knew East was waiting for a spade ruff.

DEAL 142   WASTE NOT, WANT NOT

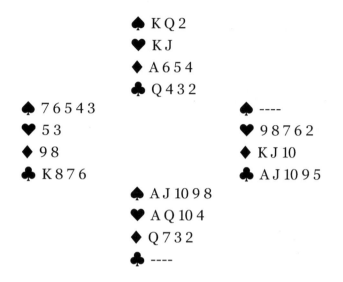

♠ K Q 2
♥ K J
♦ A 6 5 4
♣ Q 4 3 2

♠ 7 6 5 4 3
♥ 5 3
♦ 9 8
♣ K 8 7 6

♠ ----
♥ 9 8 7 6 2
♦ K J 10
♣ A J 10 9 5

♠ A J 10 9 8
♥ A Q 10 4
♦ Q 7 3 2
♣ ----

Contract: 4 ♠

Opening Lead: ♣ 6

Declarer ruffed the opening lead. Relieved for once that he had good trump spots and didn't have to worry about a 4/1 split, declarer led the spade eight to the king. East showed out.

Well, he was right; he didn't have to worry about a 4/1 but hadn't thought about a 5/0. So drawing trumps was out. West would have more trumps than South. Declarer cashed the diamond ace, then the king and ace of hearts and led a heart.

West played the spade three. So declarer was only getting one heart ruff. Nine tricks. Down one.

Could declarer have assured his contract against even a 5/0 split?

He can count five spade tricks in hand, two high hearts, and the diamond ace. If he can ruff two of his high hearts with high trumps, that's ten.

Just don't waste that spade king at the beginning.

DEAL 143   SPOT CARDS MEAN A LOT

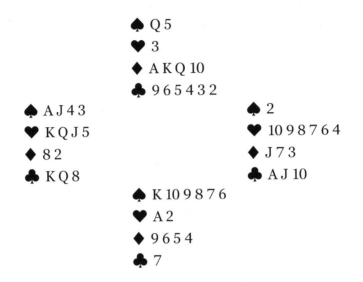

Contract: 4 ♠ Doubled

Opening Lead: ♥ King

Mike Lawrence showed this theme in the "ACBL Bulletin" some years ago.

Declarer won the opening lead and ruffed a heart. Then came the spade queen, ducked. Trying to get to his hand to draw trumps, declarer played a club. East won the ace and played a heart. South ruffed and led a low spade to West's jack. Another heart ruffed by declarer. Now West had ♠A4 and declare ♠K10.

South was done. If he led another spade, West would make him ruff again, setting up the spade four as the setting trick and probably one other trick.

Do you see Mike's solution to get ahead of the defense?

An unusual safety play. Win the opening lead. Then ruff a heart in dummy low and lead the ♠Q to the ♠K. Or ruff high and lead a spade to the ten.

Either way with that spade suit, South will win the race to the finish line.

DEAL 144 WHO TO BLAME?

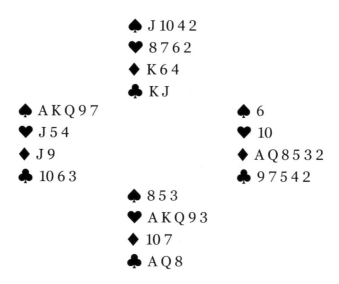

```
                    ♠ J 10 4 2
                    ♥ 8 7 6 2
                    ♦ K 6 4
                    ♣ K J
        ♠ A K Q 9 7              ♠ 6
        ♥ J 5 4                  ♥ 10
        ♦ J 9                    ♦ A Q 8 5 3 2
        ♣ 10 6 3                 ♣ 9 7 5 4 2
                    ♠ 8 5 3
                    ♥ A K Q 9 3
                    ♦ 10 7
                    ♣ A Q 8
```

West	North	East	South
P	P	P	1♥
1♠	2♥	All Pass	

Opening Lead: ♠ Ace

West started with the ♠AKQ. East followed once, then played the eight and five of diamonds. West played a fourth spade, East ruffing with the ♥10. Declarer overruffed and turned eight tricks into seven.

West's ♥J became the setting trick.

Who should we blame for the result, West or South?

Both. South knows the diamond ace is offside. West is a passed hand. Instead of overruffing, he should discard a diamond, protecting his eight tricks.

But West, instead of the fourth spade, can still get his trump promotion. East tried to get a diamond switch.

If West switches to the jack of diamonds at Trick 4, now three rounds of diamonds and declarer is helpless to prevent the trump promotion.

DEAL 145   DRAWING TRUMPS, HIGH OR LOW?

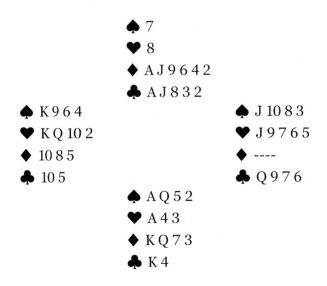

```
                    ♠ 7
                    ♥ 8
                    ♦ A J 9 6 4 2
                    ♣ A J 8 3 2
    ♠ K 9 6 4                    ♠ J 10 8 3
    ♥ K Q 10 2                   ♥ J 9 7 6 5
    ♦ 10 8 5                     ♦ ----
    ♣ 10 5                       ♣ Q 9 7 6
                    ♠ A Q 5 2
                    ♥ A 4 3
                    ♦ K Q 7 3
                    ♣ K 4
```

Contract: 7 ♦

Opening Lead: ♥ King

After an exhausting auction, North-South reach a good grand slam. Can anything go wrong? Declarer cashed the diamond king, a seemingly logical play. East showed out.

Declarer could not draw two more rounds of trumps since he needed to set up the clubs and might need two ruffs. So he played the ♣AK and ruffed a club. West overruffed.

If you thought about a 3/0 trump split, how could you overcome it?

Start the trumps by cashing the ace instead of the king. Now you can ruff clubs high twice and later lead towards dummy's ♦ J 8.

If East started with ♦1085 of trumps, you would still be safe.

DEAL 146   WHICH WAY ARE YOU GOING?

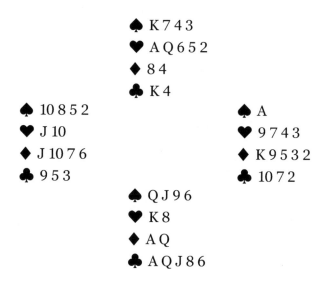

♠ K 7 4 3
♥ A Q 6 5 2
♦ 8 4
♣ K 4

♠ 10 8 5 2
♥ J 10
♦ J 10 7 6
♣ 9 5 3

♠ A
♥ 9 7 4 3
♦ K 9 5 3 2
♣ 10 7 2

♠ Q J 9 6
♥ K 8
♦ A Q
♣ A Q J 8 6

Contract: 6 ♠

Opening Lead: ♦ Jack

After the favorable opening lead, declarer led a spade to the king. Painful, down one.

Was there a better (safer) way to play?

Another declarer thought about possible bad splits. What if someone has a singleton ace? If East does, declarer must lead towards her hand.

If there is a singleton ace with West, declarer can still handle ♠10852 in the East. If West started with ♠A1082, unlucky, not your day.

So go to dummy to start the trumps.

DEAL 147   THREE OPTIONS

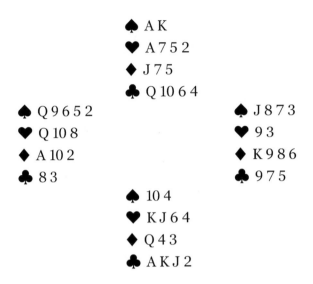

♠ A K
♥ A 7 5 2
♦ J 7 5
♣ Q 10 6 4

♠ Q 9 6 5 2
♥ Q 10 8
♦ A 10 2
♣ 8 3

♠ J 8 7 3
♥ 9 3
♦ K 9 8 6
♣ 9 7 5

♠ 10 4
♥ K J 6 4
♦ Q 4 3
♣ A K J 2

Contract: 4 ♥
Opening Lead: ♠ 5

Declarer won the spade ace and played a heart to the ace, both opponents following small. He led a small heart from dummy, East played small, declarer played the jack and West won the queen. West played another spade.

After drawing the last trump and cashing the clubs, declarer finally realized this hand was about the diamonds, not the trumps. He lost three diamond tricks, down one.

Eight ever, nine never, or was four hearts cold with 3/2 trumps?

The other declarer saw the problem as a bridge hand. The last thing she wanted to do was be the one to start the diamonds. So cash the A-K of trumps. When both follow, the hand is over.

Cash the other high spade, cash the good clubs. If someone ruffs in, they have to either 1) break the diamond suit, or 2) present declarer with a ruff/sluff, taking care of one of the diamond losers. Otherwise, declarer can exit a heart, same result.

If the trump queen fell under the king, then you would lose no hearts, but you would lose three diamonds. Four hearts is cold with or without a trump loser.

DEAL 148   MORE OPTIONS

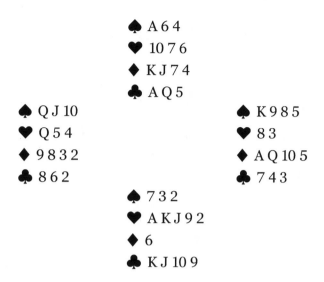

♠ A 6 4
♥ 10 7 6
♦ K J 7 4
♣ A Q 5

♠ Q J 10   ♠ K 9 8 5
♥ Q 5 4   ♥ 8 3
♦ 9 8 3 2   ♦ A Q 10 5
♣ 8 6 2   ♣ 7 4 3

♠ 7 3 2
♥ A K J 9 2
♦ 6
♣ K J 10 9

Contract: 4 ♥

Opening Lead: ♠ Queen

Declarer won the opening lead and took a trump finesse. He lost two spades, one heart, and one diamond. That was quick, not much of an effort.

Is there a way to combine your chances to make four hearts?

For starters, duck the opening lead and win the second spade. Cash the A-K of trumps; if the queen falls (some days it does), problem over. OK, so not today.

But you are still alive. Cash three rounds of clubs, everyone follows and lead the last high club.

What can West do? You discard your spade loser if he does or does not ruff. Losing one spade, one diamond, and one trump.

DEAL 149 DRAWING TRUMPS: HOW TO START

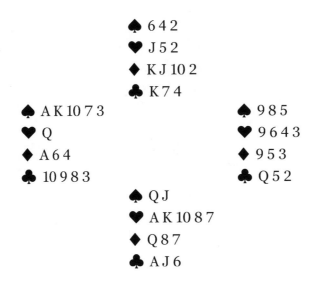

♠ 6 4 2
♥ J 5 2
♦ K J 10 2
♣ K 7 4

♠ A K 10 7 3
♥ Q
♦ A 6 4
♣ 10 9 8 3

♠ 9 8 5
♥ 9 6 4 3
♦ 9 5 3
♣ Q 5 2

♠ Q J
♥ A K 10 8 7
♦ Q 8 7
♣ A J 6

South	West	North	East
1♥	1♠	2♥	P
3♦	P	4♥	All Pass

Opening Lead: ♠ Ace

West leads the spade ace, then king, and a third, South ruffing. Still missing the diamond ace, he needs to bring in the heart suit for no losers.

He went to dummy with a club and took a losing heart finesse.

Should declarer have started with the ace? A previous hand said no.

Every hand is different. This suit has better spots. Yes, play the ace. But now since you know East has four, what do you have to do?

Right, establish the side suit, diamonds, while there is still a high trump in dummy to take care of another spade. Then declarer can finesse East's trumps.

164

DEAL 150   WHO CARES?

♠ ----
♥ K 7 3
♦ K Q 9 6
♣ K J 8 7 5 2

♠ 10 7 6 3
♥ A J 10 9 6 2
♦ ----
♣ A Q 3

Contract: 6 ♥
Opening Lead: ♠ Ace

Declarer ruffed the opening lead. Looked like a lot of tricks, but when he cashed the A-K of hearts, no queen. Twist and squirm, try as he could, there was no way to bring home twelve tricks. He couldn't get rid of all those spades.

How should declarer have played?

As long as trumps are 2/2 or any 3/1, slam is there waiting. All declarer has to do at Trick 2 is take a trump finesse not caring if it wins or loses, just get the darn queen out.

Lead a small heart from dummy and finesse.

1) It wins. Play to the king of hearts, ruff a diamond, draw trumps.
2) It loses. Do the same thing, winning any return and draw trumps.

Just anything but cashing the A-K.

The East/West hands? Put the queen wherever you like.

DEAL 151   CAN'T TRUST ANYONE THESE DAYS

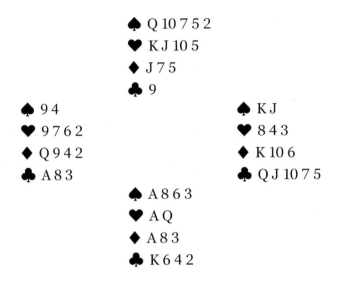

♠ Q 10 7 5 2
♥ K J 10 5
♦ J 7 5
♣ 9

♠ 9 4
♥ 9 7 6 2
♦ Q 9 4 2
♣ A 8 3

♠ K J
♥ 8 4 3
♦ K 10 6
♣ Q J 10 7 5

♠ A 8 6 3
♥ A Q
♦ A 8 3
♣ K 6 4 2

Contract: 4 ♠

Opening Lead: ♦ 2

Declarer won the opening lead. Faced with lots of losers he decided to cash the spade ace, then play hearts discarding diamonds.

He played the spade ace, East played the king. Hearts were 4/3. Declarer went down one.

What happened?

East was bridge expert and famous columnist Frank Stewart. After the first trump play, the king falling, declarer decided to change plans.

He led a spade to the ten, Frank won the jack. He cashed two diamonds and a club for down one.

Well done, Frank!

DEAL 152   YOU ARE NOT HARRY

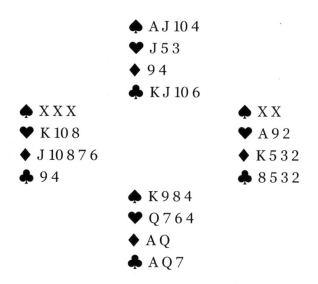

♠ A J 10 4
♥ J 5 3
♦ 9 4
♣ K J 10 6

♠ X X X
♥ K 10 8
♦ J 10 8 7 6
♣ 9 4

♠ X X
♥ A 9 2
♦ K 5 3 2
♣ 8 5 3 2

♠ K 9 8 4
♥ Q 7 6 4
♦ A Q
♣ A Q 7

Contract: 4 ♠
Opening Lead: ♦ Jack

Declarer received a favorable opening lead. He had eight trumps and tried to guess the trump queen. He misguessed and later lost three heart tricks.

Down one.

Was declarer too much of a slave to nursery rhymes?

Yes. There is a much better line of play. Unless your name is Harry Stappenbeck, 6 feet, 11 inches tall, don't try guessing the queen here.

Cash the ♠AK. Hey, the queen might drop. Assuming it did not, cash the ♦A, then run clubs discarding a heart.

If no one has ruffed in, give up a trump. That player has to break the heart suit or give you a ruff/sluff. This line only needs 3/2 trumps.

DEAL 153   COMES WITH A GUARANTEE

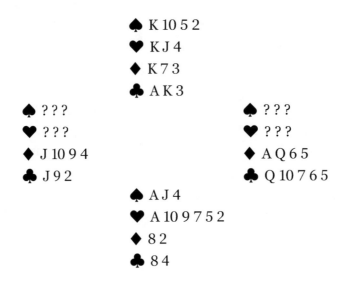

♠ K 10 5 2
♥ K J 4
♦ K 7 3
♣ A K 3

♠ ? ? ?
♥ ? ? ?
♦ J 10 9 4
♣ J 9 2

♠ ? ? ?
♥ ? ? ?
♦ A Q 6 5
♣ Q 10 7 6 5

♠ A J 4
♥ A 10 9 7 5 2
♦ 8 2
♣ 8 4

Contract: 4 ♥

Opening Lead: ♦ Jack

Declarer ruffs the third diamond and has potential losers in both majors. On a bad day, down one. Cash the ♥AK? You have nine.

Is there a way to guarantee the contract?

Yes. Play the ♣AK and ruff a club. Now cash the ♥A. You have nine trumps, but if you play a heart to the jack and East wins, he is endplayed.

He must play a spade or give you a ruff/sluff, losing at most two diamonds and one trump.

DEAL 154 BOTH TO BLAME

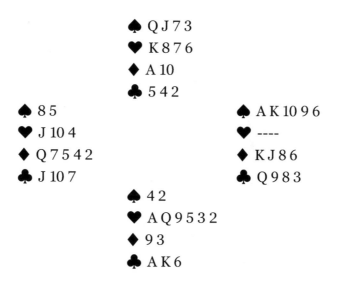

```
                    ♠ Q J 7 3
                    ♥ K 8 7 6
                    ♦ A 10
                    ♣ 5 4 2
     ♠ 8 5                        ♠ A K 10 9 6
     ♥ J 10 4                     ♥ ----
     ♦ Q 7 5 4 2                  ♦ K J 8 6
     ♣ J 10 7                     ♣ Q 9 8 3
                    ♠ 4 2
                    ♥ A Q 9 5 3 2
                    ♦ 9 3
                    ♣ A K 6
```

Contract: 4 ♥ (East overcalls in spades)

Opening Lead: ♠ 8

East won the first two tricks and continued with a third spade. Declarer ruffed with the trump queen. When trumps broke 3/0, declarer had a trump loser.

Declarer had one discard on the high spade, but she still lost one minor trick in the end.

Could declarer have done better? What about East's defense?

East was trying to let declarer make four hearts and declarer failed to take advantage of the poor defense.

After East played a third spade, South should just discard a minor loser rather than get into a losing trump fight. Now she can draw trumps and throw away the other loser on the high spade.

But East was to blame. After winning the first spade and switching to a club, South has no chance. Setting up winners for declarer is rarely the right defense.

DEAL 155   AVOIDING PROBLEMS

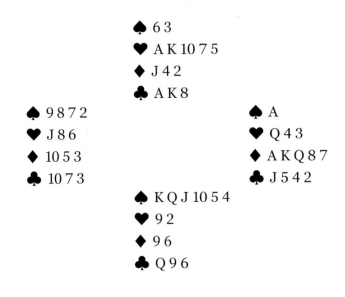

```
                       ♠ 6 3
                       ♥ A K 10 7 5
                       ♦ J 4 2
                       ♣ A K 8
       ♠ 9 8 7 2                      ♠ A
       ♥ J 8 6                        ♥ Q 4 3
       ♦ 10 5 3                       ♦ A K Q 8 7
       ♣ 10 7 3                       ♣ J 5 4 2
                       ♠ K Q J 10 5 4
                       ♥ 9 2
                       ♦ 9 6
                       ♣ Q 9 6
```

North	East	South	West
1♥	2♦	3♠	P
4♠	All Pass		

Opening Lead: ♦ 3

East won the ♦AK and played a third round. West followed so he probably had started with three. Declarer ruffed low. So far so good. But the danger was lurking. Declarer started to draw trumps now by leading the king,

East won the ace as expected and led another diamond. Now the danger raised its head. West had started with four trumps to the nine and was getting another trump trick. Down one.

What did declarer forget to consider?

What could go wrong? Declarer had to cater to the possibility of East's probable spade ace being a singleton. He could simply go to dummy to start the trumps.

Up pops the ace. Hand over; declarer can now afford to ruff the fourth diamond high.

DEAL 156   AVOIDING TROUBLE

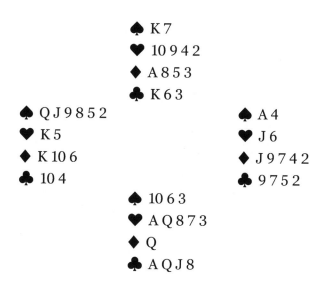

```
                    ♠ K 7
                    ♥ 10 9 4 2
                    ♦ A 8 5 3
                    ♣ K 6 3
    ♠ Q J 9 8 5 2              ♠ A 4
    ♥ K 5                      ♥ J 6
    ♦ K 10 6                   ♦ J 9 7 4 2
    ♣ 10 4                     ♣ 9 7 5 2
                    ♠ 10 6 3
                    ♥ A Q 8 7 3
                    ♦ Q
                    ♣ A Q J 8
```

West	North	East	South
2♠	P	P	3♥
P	4♥	All Pass	

Opening Lead: ♠ Queen

Declarer has two spade losers so the problem is to hold the trump losers to one. The danger of an overruff also exists. One declarer played the spade king, East won the ace and retuned the suit.

Declarer ruffed the third round, but East overruffed, down one.

Could this have been avoided?

At the other table declarer ducked the opening lead, blocking the spade suit. East couldn't afford to overtake at Trick 1. Declarer won the next trick, played the hearts as safely as possible by cashing the ace first, holding the trump losses to one.

DEAL 157   SAFETY FIRST

♠ K 10 9 8 5
♥ 7 3 2
♦ A 7
♣ 8 4 2

♠ Q
♥ A K J 9 6 5 4
♦ 9 3
♣ A K 6

Contract: 4 ♥
Opening Lead: ♦ King

At one table in a team game, declarer won the opening lead and played a trump to her ace. When West showed out, she lost a trick in each suit.

When comparing with her teammates, she found the other declarer made four hearts by taking a first round heart finesse.

Why would the other declarer take such an anti-percentage play?

It was a 100% safety play if East had three hearts. If West had ♥Q108, there was nothing she could do. But she could assure the contract by taking the finesse against East.

If it lost to the queen, she had a heart entry to the spade king. She could play the spade queen, then throw the club loser on the spade king.

DEAL 158   EITHER WAY WORKS

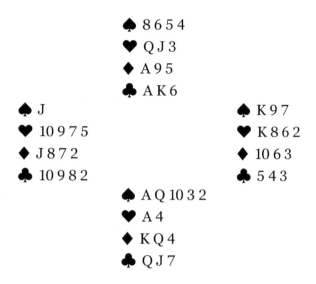

♠ 8 6 5 4
♥ Q J 3
♦ A 9 5
♣ A K 6

♠ J
♥ 10 9 7 5
♦ J 8 7 2
♣ 10 9 8 2

♠ K 9 7
♥ K 8 6 2
♦ 10 6 3
♣ 5 4 3

♠ A Q 10 3 2
♥ A 4
♦ K Q 4
♣ Q J 7

Contract: 6 ♠
Opening Lead: ♣ 10

One declarer won the opening lead in dummy and led a spade. East played the seven. Declarer stared at the ceiling for awhile, nothing appeared, and he then played the ten losing to the jack. Another club came back.

He led another spade, East played the nine, declarer looked up, again no help from above, and went up with the ace. West showed out. Down one. A loud thunderbolt came down now from somewhere above. I think it was from North.

How would you have played the trump suit and the hand?

One has to look at the whole hand. How many trump tricks can you afford to lose? It depends. Is there a heart loser or not? Take the heart finesse first. It wins!

So now you want to play spades as safely as possible for one loser.

Cash the ace, planning on going to dummy to lead another spade. The jack falls under the ace. Knock out the spade king and all is well. If you could not have afforded a spade loser, you would have started low to the queen.

Notice you make six spades if the heart finesse wins or loses.

DEAL 159   NO WAY

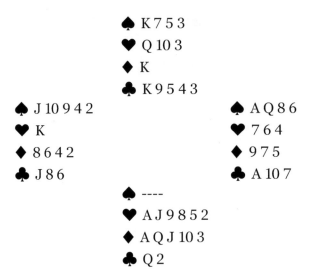

♠ K 7 5 3
♥ Q 10 3
♦ K
♣ K 9 5 4 3

♠ J 10 9 4 2
♥ K
♦ 8 6 4 2
♣ J 8 6

♠ A Q 8 6
♥ 7 6 4
♦ 9 7 5
♣ A 10 7

♠ ----
♥ A J 9 8 5 2
♦ A Q J 10 3
♣ Q 2

North	South
P	1♥
1♠	2♦
3♥	5♥
5NT	6♥
P	

Opening Lead: ♠ Jack

Declarer ruffed the opening lead. He went to dummy with a diamond and took a losing heart finesse. Down one.

At the other table declarer played a heart to her ace. Why?

At the other table, declarer was not quite ready to play trumps. She played a club first. Clubs? Why?

A discovery play. When East turned up with the ♣A, and from the opening lead the ♠AQ, there is no way East as a passed hand can have the ♥K.

So declarer's best play is the ace and hope to get lucky. Making six hearts.

DEAL 160   TRUMPS ARE MADE FOR TRUMPING

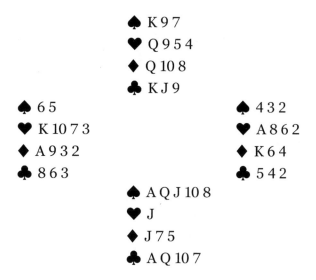

♠ K 9 7
♥ Q 9 5 4
♦ Q 10 8
♣ K J 9

♠ 6 5
♥ K 10 7 3
♦ A 9 3 2
♣ 8 6 3

♠ 4 3 2
♥ A 8 6 2
♦ K 6 4
♣ 5 4 2

♠ A Q J 10 8
♥ J
♦ J 7 5
♣ A Q 10 7

Contract: 4 ♠

Opening Lead: ♥ 3

Declarer ruffed the second heart and could only count nine tricks. If he drew three rounds of trumps, even with a friendly 3-2 split, he would never be able to establish a diamond trick. After much agonizing, he went quietly down one.

When comparing, the other declarer had made four spades. How?

The other declarer saw the futility of Plan A, trying to establish a diamond trick. So she went to Plan B. Accept the force (sounds like Star Wars) and try for a dummy reversal.

Ruff the second heart high and lead the ♠8 to the ♠9 in dummy. Ruff another heart, then cross to the ♠K in dummy and ruff the last heart.

Yes, declarer is out of trumps but not out of control. She can go to dummy with a club. The ♠7 is high to draw the last trump, discarding a diamond. That's game, Mr. Ten tricks.

That's why they call them trumps.

DEAL 161   MORE TRUMPS FOR TRUMPING

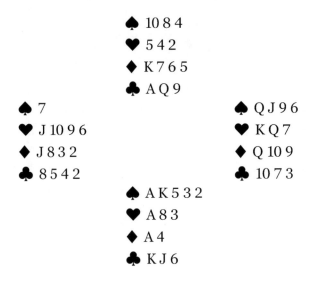

♠ 10 8 4
♥ 5 4 2
♦ K 7 6 5
♣ A Q 9

♠ 7   ♠ Q J 9 6
♥ J 10 9 6   ♥ K Q 7
♦ J 8 3 2   ♦ Q 10 9
♣ 8 5 4 2   ♣ 10 7 3

♠ A K 5 3 2
♥ A 8 3
♦ A 4
♣ K J 6

Contract: 4 ♠
Opening Lead: ♥ Jack

One declarer won the opening lead and played the ♠AK. Making no effort, he played another trump, down one.

Another declarer was + 620 in 4♠. How?

Trumps are for trumping, we just went thru this. After discovering the bad break, declarer played the ♦AK and ruffed a diamond. She played three rounds of clubs, ending in the dummy and led another diamond.

She had won nine tricks at this point, to reach this position, North on lead:

North: ♠ 10 ♥ 5 4 ♦ 7 ♣ --

East: ♠ Q J ♥ K Q ♦ -- ♣ --

South: ♠ 5 3 ♥ 8 3 ♦ -- ♣ --

East is helpless. South can't be prevented from scoring one more trump trick 'en passant'. If East ruffs, South discards and the other way around.

DEAL 162   JUST DO IT AGAIN

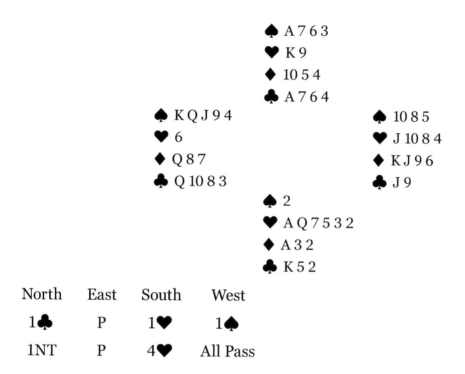

```
            ♠ A 7 6 3
            ♥ K 9
            ♦ 10 5 4
            ♣ A 7 6 4
♠ K Q J 9 4              ♠ 10 8 5
♥ 6                     ♥ J 10 8 4
♦ Q 8 7                 ♦ K J 9 6
♣ Q 10 8 3              ♣ J 9
            ♠ 2
            ♥ A Q 7 5 3 2
            ♦ A 3 2
            ♣ K 5 2
```

North	East	South	West
1♣	P	1♥	1♠
1NT	P	4♥	All Pass

Opening Lead: ♠ King

Declarer won the opening lead and started to draw trumps. There would be no problem if trumps divided 3-2, but of course, the inevitable happened. He ended down one.

Just the usual "bad luck" or would you have looked ahead?

Another declarer saw the only problem could be a 4-1 trump split. She made the good play of ruffing a spade at Trick 2. She cashed the ace, then the king of trumps. Had the trumps split 3-2, she could claim.

When West showed out, she ruffed another spade. Declarer cashed the ♥Q, ♦A, ♣K, and led a club to dummy's ♣A.

This was the position with the lead in the North hand:

North: ♠ 3 ♥ -- ♦ 10 5 ♣ 7

East: ♠ -- ♥ J ♦ K J 9 ♣ --

South: ♠ -- ♥ 7 ♦ 3 2 ♣ 5

Declarer led dummy's last spade. East could not prevent South from scoring her last small trump 'en passant' for her tenth trick.

DEAL 163   DON'T GIVE UP

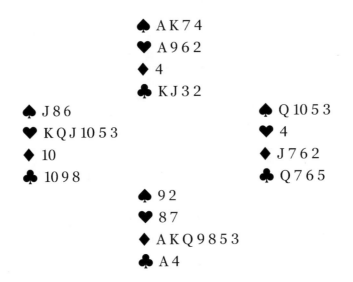

♠ A K 7 4
♥ A 9 6 2
♦ 4
♣ K J 3 2

♠ J 8 6
♥ K Q J 10 5 3
♦ 10
♣ 10 9 8

♠ Q 10 5 3
♥ 4
♦ J 7 6 2
♣ Q 7 6 5

♠ 9 2
♥ 8 7
♦ A K Q 9 8 5 3
♣ A 4

Contract: 6 ♦   (West preempts in hearts)
Opening Lead: ♥ King

Declarer wins the heart ace and cashes the A-K of trumps, West showing out on the second round.

Must South lose a heart and a diamond?

Declarer saw several possible solutions. She played the ♣AK and a club ruff. The queen did not fall. Now a spade to the dummy and ruff the last club. One more spade to the dummy and a spade ruff.

Now declarer's trump holding was reduced to ♦Q9, the same length as East. At this point, declarer exited a heart. South had ♦Q9, East had ♦J7.

West's heart return left East in an impossible position. A trump coup.
Making six diamonds.

DEAL 164   HOW TO PLAY THE TRUMPS?

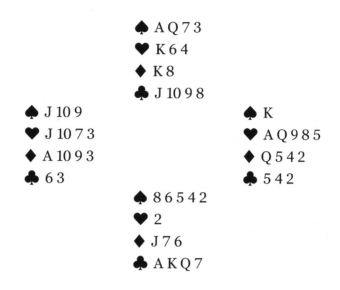

♠ A Q 7 3
♥ K 6 4
♦ K 8
♣ J 10 9 8

♠ J 10 9
♥ J 10 7 3
♦ A 10 9 3
♣ 6 3

♠ K
♥ A Q 9 8 5
♦ Q 5 4 2
♣ 5 4 2

♠ 8 6 5 4 2
♥ 2
♦ J 7 6
♣ A K Q 7

North	East	South	West
1♣	1♥	1♠	2♥
2♠	P	4♠	All Pass

Opening Lead: ♥ Jack

Declarer ruffed the second heart and led a spade to the queen. East won and led the heart ace. When West showed up with the diamond ace, South was only down one.

At the other table, that same declarer dropped another king. Why?

Again a bit of a discovery play. The way to play the trumps depends on how many spade losers declarer can afford. Well, how many diamond losers do you have?
So first lead a diamond. When West shows up with the ace, South can play spades as safely as possible, cashing the ace first.

If declarer had two diamond losers, and could not afford a spade loser, then you would have to play West for ♠Kx of spades.

179

DEAL 165   FINESSE OR NOT?

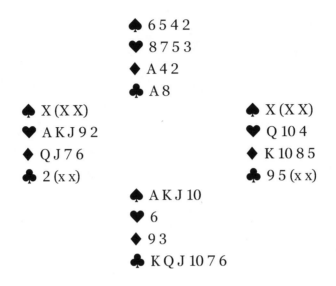

♠ 6 5 4 2
♥ 8 7 5 3
♦ A 4 2
♣ A 8

♠ X (X X)
♥ A K J 9 2
♦ Q J 7 6
♣ 2 (x x)

♠ X (X X)
♥ Q 10 4
♦ K 10 8 5
♣ 9 5 (x x)

♠ A K J 10
♥ 6
♦ 9 3
♣ K Q J 10 7 6

South	West	North	East
1♣	1♥	Dbl	2♥
3♠	P	4♠	All Pass

Opening Lead: ♥ Ace

West played the ♥AK, declarer ruffing the second round. Declarer has to decide how to play the trump suit. He could cash the top trumps and start the clubs.

Or he could cash one high one and go to dummy to take a finesse.

What's it going to be?

If you start from the top and trumps are 3/2, no problem. What about taking a finesse? If either East or West has four spades to the queen you are going down.

The worse case is if you take a finesse and it loses you will have to ruff another heart. That will set up a second spade trick for the defense.

Playing from the top is the best bet most of the time.

DEAL 166   YOU HAVE OPTIONS

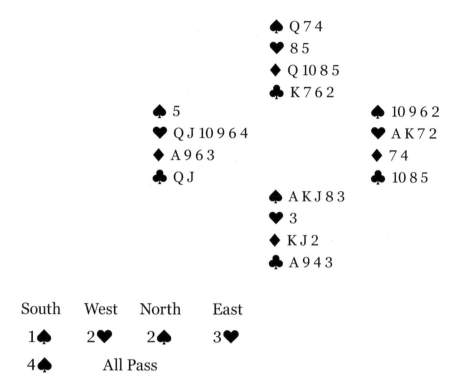

♠ Q 7 4
♥ 8 5
♦ Q 10 8 5
♣ K 7 6 2

♠ 5
♥ Q J 10 9 6 4
♦ A 9 6 3
♣ Q J

♠ 10 9 6 2
♥ A K 7 2
♦ 7 4
♣ 10 8 5

♠ A K J 8 3
♥ 3
♦ K J 2
♣ A 9 4 3

South	West	North	East
1♠	2♥	2♠	3♥
4♠	All Pass		

Opening Lead: ♥ Queen

Declarer ruffed the second round of hearts. After drawing trumps, and having none left, he cashed two good clubs, but when he played a diamond, it was all over, but counting the undertricks.

The problem of control is the same. The solution is a little different.

Another declarer saw that it didn't matter which tricks he took, as long as they added up to ten. At Trick 2 instead of ruffing, she discarded a club.

She won the club shift and drew trumps. The other club later went away on the long diamond in dummy.

DEAL 167   IF ALL ELSE FAILS

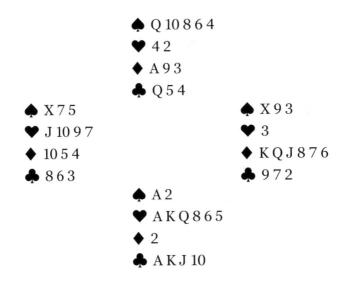

♠ Q 10 8 6 4
♥ 4 2
♦ A 9 3
♣ Q 5 4

♠ X 7 5
♥ J 10 9 7
♦ 10 5 4
♣ 8 6 3

♠ X 9 3
♥ 3
♦ K Q J 8 7 6
♣ 9 7 2

♠ A 2
♥ A K Q 8 6 5
♦ 2
♣ A K J 10

Contract: 6 ♥ (After East opens 2♦, weak)
Opening Lead: ♦ 4

The contract looked pretty good. Declarer won the opening lead. When trumps broke 4-1, he conceded a spade trick for down one. Not much of an effort.

Could you have done better?

Another declarer at least gave it a try. It should be possible to endplay West with a trump to break the spade suit. Win the ♦A and ruff a diamond. After cashing three high hearts, go to the ♣Q and ruff another diamond.

Now lead clubs. If West ruffs in, he will have nothing left but spades. If he does not ruff in, play a heart yourself.

OK, now you have to guess the spade. Who has the king? Who has the jack? But at least you have a good chance. But having come this far, I'm sure you will get it right. Well played!

DEAL 168   NO GUESSING NEEDED

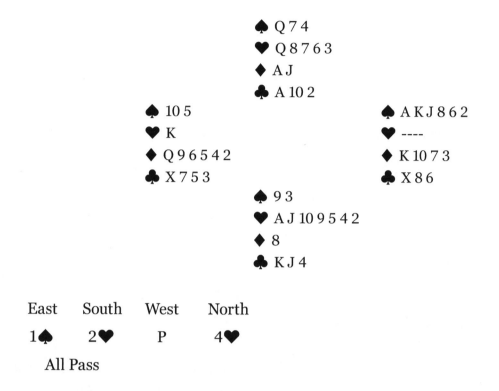

```
                        ♠ Q 7 4
                        ♥ Q 8 7 6 3
                        ♦ A J
                        ♣ A 10 2
        ♠ 10 5                          ♠ A K J 8 6 2
        ♥ K                             ♥ ----
        ♦ Q 9 6 5 4 2                   ♦ K 10 7 3
        ♣ X 7 5 3                       ♣ X 8 6
                        ♠ 9 3
                        ♥ A J 10 9 5 4 2
                        ♦ 8
                        ♣ K J 4
```

East	South	West	North
1♠	2♥	P	4♥

All Pass

Opening Lead: ♠ 10

East won two rounds of spades and continued a third round. South considered discarding a club which would succeed if East had the heart king. He rejected the idea, and ruffed with the trump jack, West overruffed and returned a diamond.

Declarer played a few rounds of trumps, but finally had to try to guess the club queen. Unlucky, down one. North started muttering about South's play.

What do you think North was muttering about?

The contract was cold, a classic elimination type hand. At the other table, the declarer realized there was no need to guess the club queen. Put the defenders to work, that's what they are there for, isn't it?

Ruff the third spade with the trump ace, play the diamond ace, and ruff a diamond. With the spades and diamonds eliminated, play a trump.

Whoever has the trump king is endplayed into giving you a ruff/sluff for a club discard or breaking the club suit. Making four hearts, no guessing needed.

DEAL 169   SAFETY FIRST

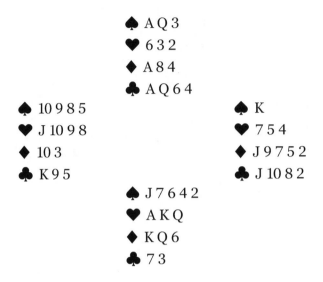

♠ A Q 3
♥ 6 3 2
♦ A 8 4
♣ A Q 6 4

♠ 10 9 8 5
♥ J 10 9 8
♦ 10 3
♣ K 9 5

♠ K
♥ 7 5 4
♦ J 9 7 5 2
♣ J 10 8 2

♠ J 7 6 4 2
♥ A K Q
♦ K Q 6
♣ 7 3

Contract: 6 ♠

Opening Lead: ♥ Jack

One declarer won the opening lead and started the trumps, low to the queen. East won the king and returned a heart. When West turned up with the ♠10985, declarer was down one, and that's with a successful club finesse.

How did the declarer at the other table make the slam? Mirrors?

There were no mirrors, but there was logical thinking. How to play the spade suit depends on the hand not just the suit. Whether the club finesse wins or loses determines the way to approach the trumps.

Another declarer took the club finesse at Trick 2, winning. Declarer can afford to lose one spade trick and need only worry about a 4-1 break, any 3-2 is no problem.

There are two losers if someone has a singleton unless the singleton is the king. So start with the ace. If both play small, play the queen and you are safe with any 3-2 break.

DEAL 170   WHO TO PLAY FOR WHAT

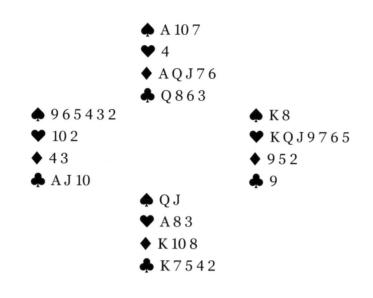

```
              ♠ A 10 7
              ♥ 4
              ♦ A Q J 7 6
              ♣ Q 8 6 3
  ♠ 9 6 5 4 3 2              ♠ K 8
  ♥ 10 2                    ♥ K Q J 9 7 6 5
  ♦ 4 3                     ♦ 9 5 2
  ♣ A J 10                  ♣ 9
              ♠ Q J
              ♥ A 8 3
              ♦ K 10 8
              ♣ K 7 5 4 2
```

South	West	North	East
1♣	P	1♦	1♥
P	P	4♣	P
5♣	All Pass		

Opening Lead: ♥ 10

With one sure club and one probable spade loser, declarer was concerned about not losing two trump tricks. From the bidding, South guessed that East was more likely to hold the club ace, so he went to dummy to lead a club to his king.

West won the ace and switched to a spade. Now the spade king rated to be with East and it was all downhill, West having started with the ♣AJ10.

Why was it better to play the trumps the other way around?

Declarer can afford to lose two trump tricks, just not a spade trick too. If the ♣Q loses to the ♣A, East can't attack spades. Declarer can win any return, play the ♣K and just keep playing diamonds.

If there is still an outstanding trump, the opponents are welcome to it anytime.

185

DEAL 171   AVOIDING THE GUESSWORK

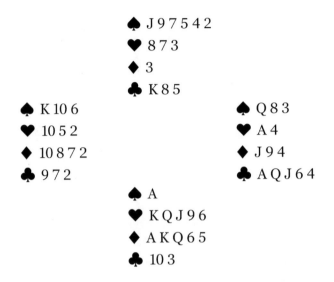

```
                        ♠ J 9 7 5 4 2
                        ♥ 8 7 3
                        ♦ 3
                        ♣ K 8 5
        ♠ K 10 6                         ♠ Q 8 3
        ♥ 10 5 2                         ♥ A 4
        ♦ 10 8 7 2                       ♦ J 9 4
        ♣ 9 7 2                          ♣ A Q J 6 4
                        ♠ A
                        ♥ K Q J 9 6
                        ♦ A K Q 6 5
                        ♣ 10 3
```

Contract: 4 ♥

Opening Lead: ♣ 2

The first trick went two, five, jack, three. East continued with the club ace and another club, West following and declarer discarding a diamond. Declarer played the diamond ace and ruffed a diamond. He now played a trump to his king, winning.

At this point he had to guess whether East started with ♥Ax or ♥Axx.

Declarer played the queen, East won the ace and led another club, promoting West's remaining ten to the setting trick.

How could this guesswork have been avoided?

Better timing. At Trick 4, lead a trump from dummy. If the king wins, now play ace and ruff a diamond.

When you lead the last trump, whether East began with two or three, he has to waste his ace on air, no guess, no trump promotion.

DEAL 172   NINE TRUMPS BUT WHAT?

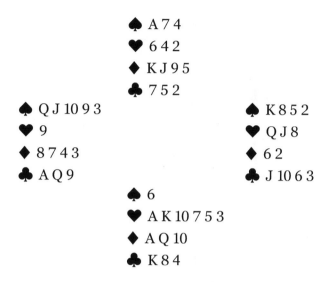

Contract: 4 ♥

Opening Lead: ♠ Queen

Declarer won the opening lead, and seeing nine trumps, began with the ace. E/W played the 8 and 9. She optimistically followed with the heart king and of course you know what happened. LHO showed out.

She started the diamonds, hoping to discard a club, but East ruffed the third diamond and played back, surprise, surprise, the club jack. Down one.

Was this a "Nine ever" or what?

This was a classic danger hand. As long as East did not get on lead, declarer was safe. So lead the first heart from dummy. If East plays the eight, insert the ten.

If West wins, the hand is over. If West follows low, go to dummy and do it again.

DEAL 173   LISTEN TO THE BIDDING

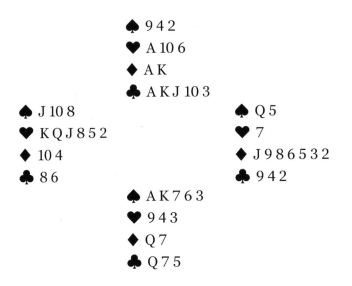

```
                        ♠ 9 4 2
                        ♥ A 10 6
                        ♦ A K
                        ♣ A K J 10 3
        ♠ J 10 8                      ♠ Q 5
        ♥ K Q J 8 5 2                 ♥ 7
        ♦ 10 4                        ♦ J 9 8 6 5 3 2
        ♣ 8 6                         ♣ 9 4 2
                        ♠ A K 7 6 3
                        ♥ 9 4 3
                        ♦ Q 7
                        ♣ Q 7 5
```

West	North	East	South
2♥	Dbl	P	4♠
P	6♠	All Pass	

Opening Lead: ♥ King

South won the opening lead, cashed two high trumps and tried to run the clubs, hoping to discard two losing hearts.

Unfortunately, West had the outstanding heart, ruffed the third club and cashed two hearts. Down two.

Could declarer have made his slam?

East is likely to have only one heart. Declarer should start trumps from dummy. If East plays low on the first round, win, go back to dummy and lead another trump. When the queen appears (or if it had on the first round), duck.

Since East has no more hearts, declarer can win the return, draw the last trump, and use the clubs.

DEAL 174   DON'T GET TAPPED OUT

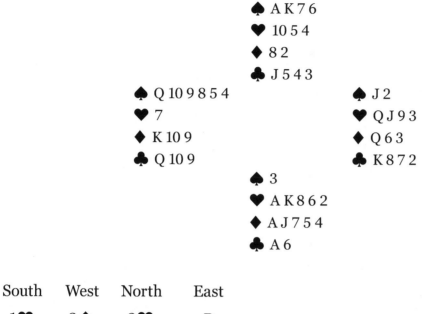

```
                        ♠ A K 7 6
                        ♥ 10 5 4
                        ♦ 8 2
                        ♣ J 5 4 3
      ♠ Q 10 9 8 5 4                    ♠ J 2
      ♥ 7                               ♥ Q J 9 3
      ♦ K 10 9                          ♦ Q 6 3
      ♣ Q 10 9                          ♣ K 8 7 2
                        ♠ 3
                        ♥ A K 8 6 2
                        ♦ A J 7 5 4
                        ♣ A 6
```

South	West	North	East
1♥	2♠	3♥	P
4♥		All Pass	

Opening Lead: ♣ 10

Declarer won the opening lead and cashed the ♠AK to discard his club. He then led ace and a low diamond. West won and led another spade. East discarding his last diamond.

South knew if he tried to ruff another diamond, East could overruff. So he cashed the ♥AK. Then South ruffed a diamond, but East discarded.

South had to ruff a club to get back to his hand. He led the high diamond. East ruffed, drew South's last trump and cashed the club king. Down one.

Too tough a split or was there a way home?

To maintain control, South plays along similar lines, but only cashes one high trump. But now he can return to his hand and just keep playing diamonds, losing two trumps and one diamond.

DEAL 175   PLEASE JUST MAKE YOUR CONTRACT

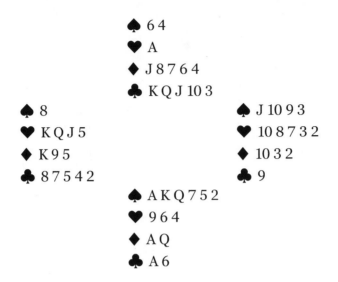

```
                    ♠ 6 4
                    ♥ A
                    ♦ J 8 7 6 4
                    ♣ K Q J 10 3
   ♠ 8                          ♠ J 10 9 3
   ♥ K Q J 5                    ♥ 10 8 7 3 2
   ♦ K 9 5                      ♦ 10 3 2
   ♣ 8 7 5 4 2                  ♣ 9
                    ♠ A K Q 7 5 2
                    ♥ 9 6 4
                    ♦ A Q
                    ♣ A 6
```

Contract: 6 ♠

Opening Lead: ♥ King

Declarer won in dummy saying "We missed a grand." North, having heard this before, cringed thinking "Please, try to make six." Declarer led a club to the ace and ruffed a heart. A diamond to the ace was followed by another heart ruff.

Declarer played the club king, intending to discard a diamond on the third club but East ruffed the club king and returned a diamond to West's king. Down one. North covered his face, trying not to say anything.

Do you think North is calling South for tomorrow's game?

This was a simple matter of hand recognition. This is a second suit hand. Why do some players insist on ruffing when they see a singleton in dummy? The contract was six, not seven.

Just duck one round of trumps at Trick 2, win any return, draw the rest of the trumps and the clubs take care of the rest of the tricks.

DEAL 176   AT THE TWO LEVEL AT LEAST MAKE IT

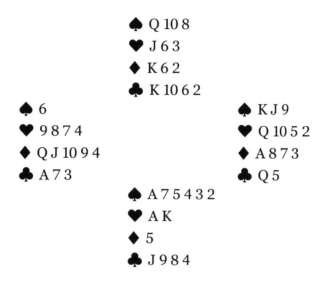

```
              ♠ Q 10 8
              ♥ J 6 3
              ♦ K 6 2
              ♣ K 10 6 2
♠ 6                         ♠ K J 9
♥ 9 8 7 4                   ♥ Q 10 5 2
♦ Q J 10 9 4                ♦ A 8 7 3
♣ A 7 3                     ♣ Q 5
              ♠ A 7 5 4 3 2
              ♥ A K
              ♦ 5
              ♣ J 9 8 4
```

Contract: 2 ♠

Opening Lead: ♦ Queen

After a quiet auction, letting N/S play in two spades, South ruffed the second diamond. He led the spade ace and a low spade. East took two spade tricks and led another diamond. Declarer next let the nine of clubs ride.

East won and led his last diamond, forcing out South's last trump. When West took the club ace, he cashed a diamond. Down one.

How can South maintain control to win eight tricks?

Another declarer realized he could afford to lose two trumps, two diamonds, and a club. He just couldn't lose control.

So after taking the ace of trumps, he started the clubs. The contract was safe.

191

DEAL 177   SIMPLE OR POSSIBLE DANGER

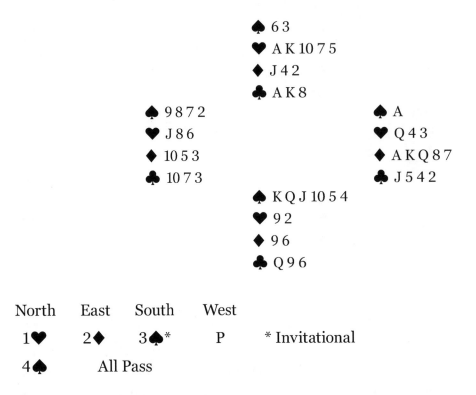

```
                    ♠ 6 3
                    ♥ A K 10 7 5
                    ♦ J 4 2
                    ♣ A K 8
      ♠ 9 8 7 2                   ♠ A
      ♥ J 8 6                     ♥ Q 4 3
      ♦ 10 5 3                    ♦ A K Q 8 7
      ♣ 10 7 3                    ♣ J 5 4 2
                    ♠ K Q J 10 5 4
                    ♥ 9 2
                    ♦ 9 6
                    ♣ Q 9 6
```

North	East	South	West
1♥	2♦	3♠*	P	* Invitational
4♠	All Pass		

Opening Lead: ♦ 3

East played the queen and king of diamonds, West following with the five. East continued with the diamond ace, South ruffed, West playing the ten.

Declarer seeing no problem, started to draw trumps and went down one.

What happened and how did another declarer avoid it?

East probably has the ace of spades. And West is out of diamonds. The first declarer started trumps by leading the king. East had the ace, but it was a singleton.

West scored a trump promotion with the ♠9872 when East played another diamond.

Another declarer foresaw the possible danger. He went to dummy with a heart and started the trumps from the board. No trump promotion.

DEAL 178   AVOIDING PROBLEMS

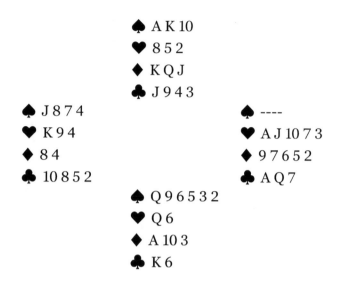

```
                      ♠ A K 10
                      ♥ 8 5 2
                      ♦ K Q J
                      ♣ J 9 4 3
        ♠ J 8 7 4                    ♠ ----
        ♥ K 9 4                      ♥ A J 10 7 3
        ♦ 8 4                        ♦ 9 7 6 5 2
        ♣ 10 8 5 2                   ♣ A Q 7
                      ♠ Q 9 6 5 3 2
                      ♥ Q 6
                      ♦ A 10 3
                      ♣ K 6
```

East	South	West	North
1♥	1♠	P	2♥
P	2♠	P	4♠
All Pass			

Opening Lead: ♥ 4

Declarer ruffed the third heart and led a trump to the ace. Seeing East show out, he came back tohis hand with the diamond ace. He led a trump to the ten, then cashed the king.

When declarer next led a club from dummy, East won the ace and led a fourth heart, promoting a trump trick for West. Down one.

How could South have managed to avoid losing a trump trick?

Play can start the same. But after playing a trump to the ten, declarer needs to leave the trump king in dummy and played a club.

Now if East puts up the ace and leads a heart, South ruffs in hand. Whether West overruffs or discards, declarer can draw trumps and make his contract.

DEAL 179 BASIC TRUMP COUP

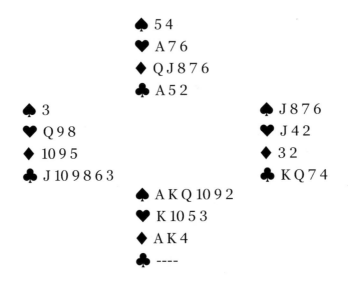

♠ 5 4
♥ A 7 6
♦ Q J 8 7 6
♣ A 5 2

♠ 3
♥ Q 9 8
♦ 10 9 5
♣ J 10 9 8 6 3

♠ J 8 7 6
♥ J 4 2
♦ 3 2
♣ K Q 7 4

♠ A K Q 10 9 2
♥ K 10 5 3
♦ A K 4
♣ ----

Contract: 7 ♠
Opening Lead: ♣ Jack

Declarer ruffed the opening lead and played the ♠AK. Can you make seven spades when West shows out?

The basics for a trump coup are to shorten your trump length to equal your RHO's trump length and lead from the dummy at the end.

Play the ace of diamonds and a low diamond to the queen. Discard the diamond king on the club ace. Lead the diamond jack. If East ruffs, declarer overruffs and has the rest.

So East discards a heart as does declarer. Another diamond, same thing. Now declarer ruffs a club to arrive at this position:

North: ♠ ---- ♥ A 7 6 ♦ 7 ♣ ----

East: ♠ J 8 ♥ J ♦ --- ♣ K

South: ♠ Q 10 ♥ K 10 ♦ ---- ♣ ----

South enters dummy with the heart ace and leads the fifth diamond. If East ruffs, overruff, draw the last trump and take the heart king.

If East discards, discard the heart king and take the last two tricks with the ♠Q10. Either way, making seven spades.

DEAL 180   CAN YOU HANDLE THIS ONE?

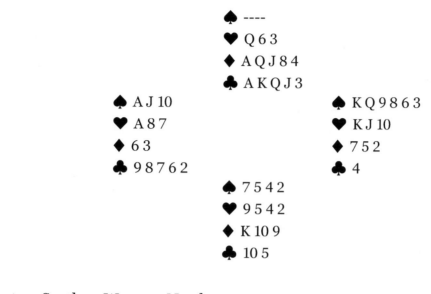

♠ ----
♥ Q 6 3
♦ A Q J 8 4
♣ A K Q J 3

♠ A J 10
♥ A 8 7
♦ 6 3
♣ 9 8 7 6 2

♠ K Q 9 8 6 3
♥ K J 10
♦ 7 5 2
♣ 4

♠ 7 5 4 2
♥ 9 5 4 2
♦ K 10 9
♣ 10 5

East	South	West	North
2♠	P	4♠	4NT
P	5♦	All Pass	

Opening Lead: ♠ Ace

After not receiving a heart lead, declarer counted his tricks. He had ten minor tricks and didn't see any hope for more. He quickly went down one.

Was there a road to eleven tricks?

Another declarer did the natural thing. He started trumping things. For once this was right!

He ruffed the opening lead, a diamond to hand, ruffed a spade high, a diamond to hand and ruffed another spade.

With no trump left in dummy, he came to his hand with the wonderful, much appreciated club ten. He played the ten of diamonds, drawing the last trump and cashed the clubs. Eleven tricks, a sort of declarer reversal.

DEAL 181 IT'S MAGIC

♠ 6 2
♥ A 8 4 2
♦ A 7
♣ A 8 6 5 2

South	North
1NT	2♣
2♥	4♥
P	

♠ Q 9 8 3   ♠ J 10 7 5
♥ Q J 10 3   ♥ 6
♦ J 10 9   ♦ 8 6 5 4 3
♣ J 10   ♣ K Q 9

Opening Lead: ♦ J

♠ A K 4
♥ K 9 7 5
♦ K Q 2
♣ 7 4 3

Declarer won the ♦A at Trick 1. He played the ♥AK. Ouch, two trump losers. With two inevitable club losers, he was down one.

Could you have pulled a David Copperfield and made one trump loser disappear?

Yes, just like the great illusionist, divert your attention elsewhere. By never touching the trumps, like the disappearing elephant, watch David make a spade loser vanish.

At Trick 2, instead of drawing trumps, cash three diamonds and one club. Then cash the ♠AK and ruff a spade. Exit with a club and East cashed his ♣KQ.

With East on lead, here is the position:

North: ♥ A 8 4
           ♣ 8

                      East: ♠ J

West: ♥ Q J 10 3   ♥ 6
                           ♦ 8 6

South: ♥ K 9 7 5

No matter what card East leads, David has limited West to one trick.
Yes, the elephant has left the building.

DEAL 182   BYE, BYE JACK

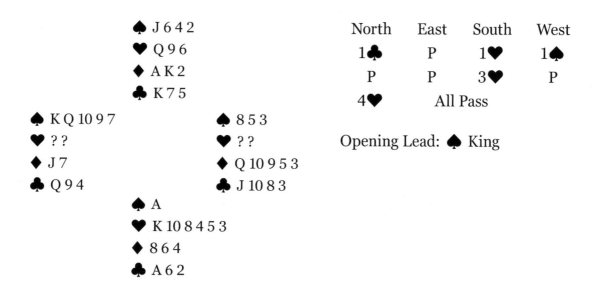

♠ J 6 4 2
♥ Q 9 6
♦ A K 2
♣ K 7 5

♠ K Q 10 9 7
♥ ? ?
♦ J 7
♣ Q 9 4

♠ 8 5 3
♥ ? ?
♦ Q 10 9 5 3
♣ J 10 8 3

♠ A
♥ K 10 8 4 5 3
♦ 8 6 4
♣ A 6 2

North	East	South	West
1♣	P	1♥	1♠
P	P	3♥	P
4♥		All Pass	

Opening Lead: ♠ King

Yes, in the diagram, East might have 14 cards, the trump suit being the unknown. Declarer won the opening lead and led a low heart to the ♥Q.

Another declarer led low to the ♥8.

But what did you do? Where is the ♥J?

The third declarer found the best way. Never touch hearts. Make the defenders break the suit. At Trick 2, cash the ♣A, and lead low to the ♣K. Ruff a spade and lead a low diamond to the ♦A. Ruff another spade and lead a low diamond to the ♦K, Ruff dummy's last spade.

With eight tricks in the bank, exit a minor loser. The defense will cash a winner in the other minor to leave:

North ♥ Q 9 6

South ♥ K 10 8

Regardless or which defender is on lead or who has what, you will not lose a trick to the ♥J.

197

DEFENSE

DEALS 183 - 221

DEAL 183   THE ACE OF TRUMPS

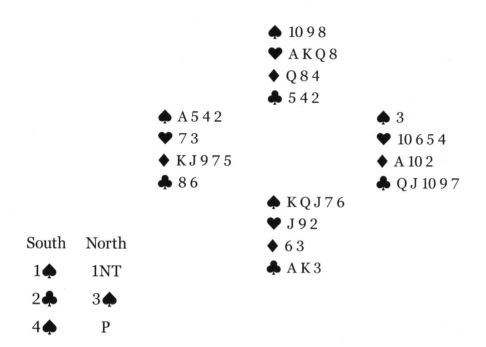

♠ 10 9 8
♥ A K Q 8
♦ Q 8 4
♣ 5 4 2

♠ A 5 4 2
♥ 7 3
♦ K J 9 7 5
♣ 8 6

♠ 3
♥ 10 6 5 4
♦ A 10 2
♣ Q J 10 9 7

♠ K Q J 7 6
♥ J 9 2
♦ 6 3
♣ A K 3

South	North
1♠	1NT
2♣	3♠
4♠	P

Opening Lead: What should West lead?

Holding four trumps to the ace, a powerful defensive holding, don't lead shortness. Not even a singleton if you had one. Your intent is to shorten South so lead your longest suit, South's likely short suit, a fourth best diamond, the seven.

East wins the ten and continues with ace and another, South ruffing. Good! Declarer now leads the spade king.

Should you take this trick?

Better not. You want to make South ruff another diamond in hand, so you have to duck the spade king and the queen. Now what?

South is in serious trouble. If he plays another spade you will win and play a diamond, forcing him to ruff with his last trump. Or he can play other suits, but then you will be ruffing. Two choices, both bad.

South leads another spade. Now you win and lead another diamond. South ruffs. Now when you ruff in, you cash your last diamond. Down two.

*** Note East's good play of the ten at Trick 1, from the Rule of Eleven.
If he had played the ace, or switched to the club queen next, South would have made four spades.

DEAL 184 ACE OF TRUMPS

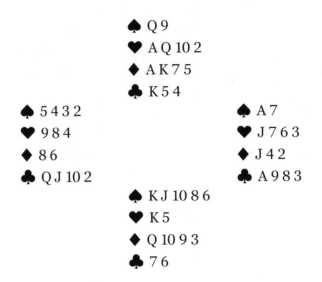

♠ Q 9
♥ A Q 10 2
♦ A K 7 5
♣ K 5 4

♠ 5 4 3 2
♥ 9 8 4
♦ 8 6
♣ Q J 10 2

♠ A 7
♥ J 7 6 3
♦ J 4 2
♣ A 9 8 3

♠ K J 10 8 6
♥ K 5
♦ Q 10 9 3
♣ 7 6

Contract: 4 ♠

Opening Lead: ♣ Queen

At one table, declarer ruffed the third club and led a spade to the queen. East won the ace and returned a trump. Declarer drew trumps and claimed.

How did declarer go down in four spades at other tables?

The play started the same, but when declarer led a spade to the queen, East ducked. South had no winning option.

If he played a second round of trumps, East would win and play another club, forcing him to ruff and lose control.

West would score the setting trick with his fourth trump.

DEAL 185   ANOTHER ACE OF TRUMPS

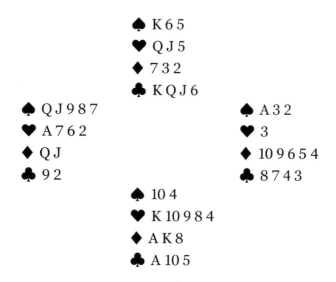

♠ K 6 5
♥ Q J 5
♦ 7 3 2
♣ K Q J 6

♠ Q J 9 8 7   ♠ A 3 2
♥ A 7 6 2   ♥ 3
♦ Q J   ♦ 10 9 6 5 4
♣ 9 2   ♣ 8 7 4 3

♠ 10 4
♥ K 10 9 8 4
♦ A K 8
♣ A 10 5

Contract: 4 ♥ (E/W bid and raise spades)
Opening Lead: ♠ Queen

West leads the spade queen, dummy plays low, and East the three (the best he can do). Now what? What is your defensive plan? Are you optimistic or not?

You have a very powerful tool. Four trumps to the ace, a very big deal. Now what?

For sure, East has the spade ace. Play the spade jack, then another spade, king, ace and South ruffs. Declarer leads the king of hearts. Are you taking this trick?

Better not. You want to win which heart? Yes, the third round, so you can continue spades forcing declarer to ruff in hand. If you win a heart before then, he can ruff in the dummy.

You win the third round, play a spade and declarer ruffs with his last trump. Guess what? Your two of hearts is the setting trick!

Had you defended in any other fashion, declarer would have made his contract, keeping control and throwing his diamond loser on the long club.

DEFENDING: DON'T TAKE THAT ACE OF TRUMPS

West   ♠ 10 9 8

♠ A 4   ♠ J 7 6

        ♠ K Q 5 3 2

Let's say the contract is four spades. You are West. Your side has taken two tricks with no future anywhere else, no rush for ruffs or anything.

Declarer goes to dummy and leads the spade ten. East plays low, declarer plays low.

What should you be thinking?

The one thing you, West, should be doing is NOT THINKING! Play the low spade as smoothly as you can.

When declarer plays trumps in this fashion, he does not have a solid suit. He is going to go back to dummy to lead the nine. Now he has a guess.

But if you sit and stare at the king for awhile before playing low, even your waiter will know you have the ace. At least give declarer a chance to go wrong.

DEAL 186   GIVE A LOSING OPTION

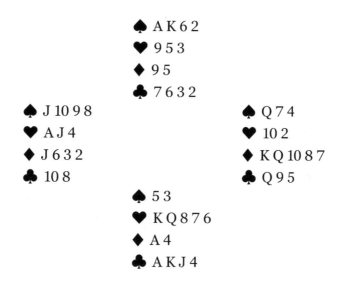

♠ A K 6 2
♥ 9 5 3
♦ 9 5
♣ 7 6 3 2

♠ J 10 9 8
♥ A J 4
♦ J 6 3 2
♣ 10 8

♠ Q 7 4
♥ 10 2
♦ K Q 10 8 7
♣ Q 9 5

♠ 5 3
♥ K Q 8 7 6
♦ A 4
♣ A K J 4

Contract: 4 ♥

Opening Lead: ♠ Jack

Declarer won the opening lead in dummy and played a trump to his king. West played low.

What should declarer do with his one remaining dummy entry?

Use it for another heart play or a club finesse? Which would you do?

Knowing when to duck a trick is an art. If West wins the first heart, South has little choice. He will probably cash the heart queen and take a winning club finesse, losing two hearts and one diamond.

On the other hand, when the heart king wins, the defense is still alive.

DEAL 187   LET THEM GO WRONG

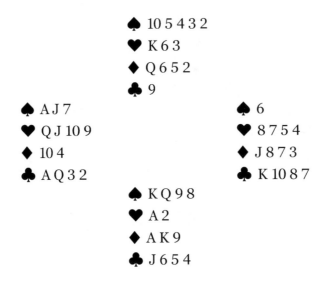

Contract: 4 ♠

Opening Lead: ♥ Queen

Declarer won the opening lead in dummy. If spades are 2/2 or the spade ace is with East, game is probably cold. Declarer led a spade to his king.

Should West win?

What's the rush? West ducked. This gave declarer a chance to do the wrong thing. At this point, he should lead a club and play along cross-ruff lines.

West cannot afford to lead spades without giving up a trump trick, but......

Declarer did do the wrong thing. He went to dummy with the diamond queen and led another spade.

Now West could play two rounds of trumps, the best defense against a cross-ruff, leaving declarer with too many losers.

DEAL 188   WIN OR DUCK?

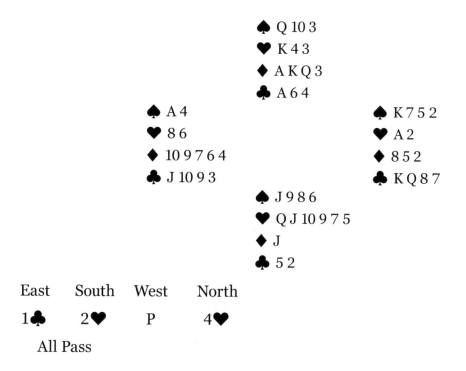

```
                        ♠ Q 10 3
                        ♥ K 4 3
                        ♦ A K Q 3
                        ♣ A 6 4
        ♠ A 4                          ♠ K 7 5 2
        ♥ 8 6                          ♥ A 2
        ♦ 10 9 7 6 4                   ♦ 8 5 2
        ♣ J 10 9 3                     ♣ K Q 8 7
                        ♠ J 9 8 6
                        ♥ Q J 10 9 7 5
                        ♦ J
                        ♣ 5 2
```

East   South   West   North

1♣   2♥   P   4♥

All Pass

Opening Lead: ♣ Jack

Declarer wins the opening lead in dummy. She plays the ace of diamonds, following with the jack. On the diamond king, she discards the club five. Now she leads the three of hearts. Your play, win or duck?

Well, we have been talking about when to take the trump ace. It's usually not right to win air on the first round. East ducked.

Declarer won the queen and played another heart. Trumps were 2/2. She still lost two spades, but make four hearts.

Could the defense have done better?

At the other table, the defender, trying to figure a way to defeat the contract, reasoned declarer is out of clubs since she could have taken another discard. So her distribution is likely 4=6=1=2. Maybe West has only two spades and the spade ace.

So she went up with the trump ace and led a low spade. If all goes well, partner will win the spade ace, return a spade to you and you can give partner a spade ruff. Down one.

DEAL 189   FORCING

North		South	North
♠ 10 9 8		1♠	1NT
♥ A K Q 8		2♣	3♠
♦ Q 8 4		4♠	P
♣ 5 4 2			

West

♠ A 5 4 2

♥ 7 3

♦ K J 9 7 5

♣ 8 6

Opening Lead: ♦ 7

East wins Trick with the ♦10, cashes the ♦A and plays a third diamond. Declarer ruffs and leads the ♠K. How should West continue the defense?

West won the ♠A and switched to the ♣8. Declarer won and finished drawing trumps. South discarded his diamond loser on dummy's long heart.

Great start, terrible stretch run. How could the defense have prevailed? The entire deal:

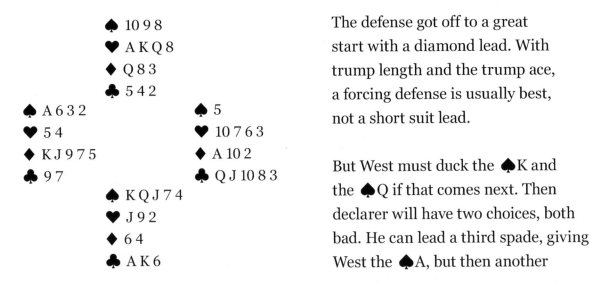

The defense got off to a great start with a diamond lead. With trump length and the trump ace, a forcing defense is usually best, not a short suit lead.

But West must duck the ♠K and the ♠Q if that comes next. Then declarer will have two choices, both bad. He can lead a third spade, giving West the ♠A, but then another

Diamond will take declarer's last trump, forcing him to lose control. Or he can start cashing outside winners but West will be ruffing.

Note East's good play at Trick 1 (♦10 from the Rule of Eleven) and diamond continuation at Trick 2, not the tempting switch to the ♣Q.)

DEAL 190   ACE OF TRUMP

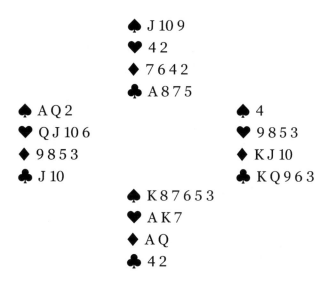

♠ J 10 9
♥ 4 2
♦ 7 6 4 2
♣ A 8 7 5

♠ A Q 2
♥ Q J 10 6
♦ 9 8 5 3
♣ J 10

♠ 4
♥ 9 8 5 3
♦ K J 10
♣ K Q 9 6 3

♠ K 8 7 6 5 3
♥ A K 7
♦ A Q
♣ 4 2

Contract: 4 ♠

Opening Lead: ♥ Queen

Declarer wins the A-K of hearts and ruffs a heart. He then leads the spade jack to West.

How should West defend?

This is a good time for a falsecard. West has two sure trump tricks but he should win the ace smoothly, not the queen. Declarer has only one dummy entry.

If you were declarer, would you use your entry to take another spade finesse, losing now to the queen, or a diamond finesse, winning?

Me, I'm taking the spade finesse, losing. What do I know? I have to find an easier game next time.

DEFENSIVE TRUMP FALSECARDING

♠ A Q 7 2

♠ 4   ♠ J 9 6 5

♠ K 10 8 3

Here is a situation that often comes up in the trump suit, but could come up anywhere.

Say, for an extreme example, the opponents bid seven spades. This is the trump suit and they have no outside losers.

Sitting East with four to the jack, can you do anything?

What's going to happen? Declarer is going to play a spade to the ace, cash the queen, see West show out, and finesse you out of your jack. Great!

But suppose you play the nine under the ace?

♠ A Q 7 2

♠ J 6 5 4   ♠ 9

♠ K 10 8 3

Now at least you have given him some losing options. He might play West for four to the jack and play low to the king next.

DEFENSIVE FALSECARDING

♠ J 9 3

♠ 8 6 5   ♠ Q 10

♠ A K 7 4 2

South is in six spades and has lost one trick. And East knows South must have the A-K of trumps and is going to get very lucky.

Where can the setting trick come from?

You can't be sure, but when South plays the ace, play the queen.

You never know. But it can't hurt and it might help.

Put a little fog in the air. You are almost surely going to score your ten.

DEAL 191   A LITTLE TRUMP SUBTREFUGE

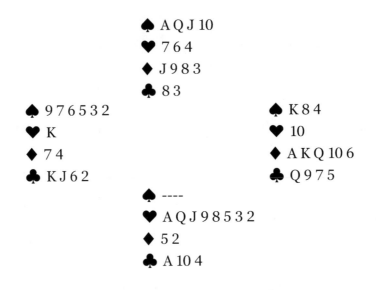

♠ A Q J 10
♥ 7 6 4
♦ J 9 8 3
♣ 8 3

♠ 9 7 6 5 3 2
♥ K
♦ 7 4
♣ K J 6 2

♠ K 8 4
♥ 10
♦ A K Q 10 6
♣ Q 9 7 5

♠ ----
♥ A Q J 9 8 5 3 2
♦ 5 2
♣ A 10 4

East	South	West	North
1♦	4♥	All Pass	

Opening Lead: ♦ 7

East won the ten of diamonds at Trick 1 and continued with the ♦AK.

Declarer ruffed with the heart nine, West overruffed with the heart king. Now declarer was able to use the trumps in dummy as entries.

Declarer took a ruffing finesse in spades against East's spade king and avoided losing a club trick, setting up the spades to discard the club losers.

How did South go down at some other tables after the same start?

When declarer ruffed the third diamond, West discarded. Placing East with the ♥K10, declarer played the ace of clubs and conceded a club.

After ruffing a club, declarer took a trump finesse. Down one.

DEAL 192   RUFF OR DON'T RUFF?

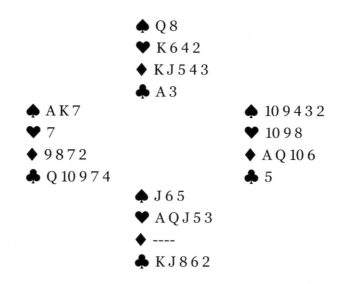

♠ Q 8
♥ K 6 4 2
♦ K J 5 4 3
♣ A 3

♠ A K 7
♥ 7
♦ 9 8 7 2
♣ Q 10 9 7 4

♠ 10 9 4 3 2
♥ 10 9 8
♦ A Q 10 6
♣ 5

♠ J 6 5
♥ A Q J 5 3
♦ ----
♣ K J 8 6 2

Contract: 4 ♥ (After a Jacoby 2NT auction, declarer shows short diamonds)
Opening Lead: ♠ Ace

West cashes two top spade tricks and switches to the diamond nine. East covers dummy's jack and South ruffs. South plays a club to the ace and leads the small club. You are East. Should you ruff?

As a general rule, when declarer leads a small card thru you, it's best not to ruff. It's called ruffing "air." Maybe something better will come along to ruff.

Let's compare ruffing and not ruffing on this hand.

Situation one: You ruff air. Declarer will get five hearts in hand, one spade, two top clubs and later two club ruffs after drawing trumps. Ten tricks.

Situation two: You don't ruff. Declarer wins five hearts in hand, one spade, two top clubs, but only one club ruff in dummy after drawing trumps. Nine tricks.

By not ruffing, you are in a position to overruff dummy, so you have reduced dummy's ruffing values by one trick. Down one.

211

DEAL 193   RUFF OR DON'T RUFF?

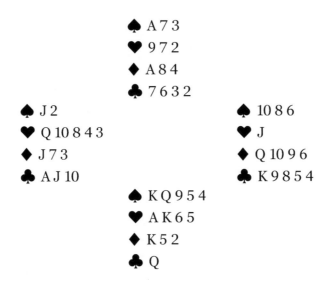

♠ A 7 3
♥ 9 7 2
♦ A 8 4
♣ 7 6 3 2

♠ J 2
♥ Q 10 8 4 3
♦ J 7 3
♣ A J 10

♠ 10 8 6
♥ J
♦ Q 10 9 6
♣ K 9 8 5 4

♠ K Q 9 5 4
♥ A K 6 5
♦ K 5 2
♣ Q

Contract: 4 ♠
Opening Lead: ♥ 4

Declarer wins trick one with the ace. At trick two, declarer leads the club queen, West wins the ace and leads the heart queen. Should you ruff?

Who has the heart king? Declarer. If West had ♥KQ, he would not have led the four. So declarer has at least three, most likely four hearts. But this would be like ruffing "air." If declarer had led low from the board, you would discard, not ruff. So it's the same here.

Situation one: If you ruff, South plays low, then draws trumps and ruffs his one heart loser. You get one trick.

Situation two: If you don't ruff, South wins the king. One heart loser goes to West's ten and he can't ruff the other heart without setting up a trump trick for you. You get two tricks.

DEAL 194   RUFF OR DON'T RUFF?

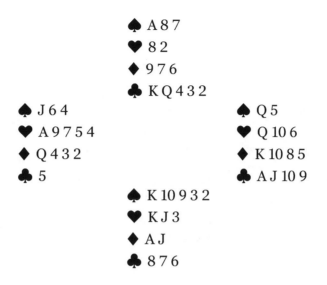

```
            ♠ A 8 7
            ♥ 8 2
            ♦ 9 7 6
            ♣ K Q 4 3 2
♠ J 6 4                    ♠ Q 5
♥ A 9 7 5 4                ♥ Q 10 6
♦ Q 4 3 2                  ♦ K 10 8 5
♣ 5                        ♣ A J 10 9
            ♠ K 10 9 3 2
            ♥ K J 3
            ♦ A J
            ♣ 8 7 6
```

South	North
1♠	1NT
2♣	3♠ (a little pushy)
P	

Opening Lead: ♣ 5 (Remember what Benito said, if you don't lead a singleton, you don't have one)

West leads his singleton, not usually a good idea in their suit, but that was the lead. It goes king, ace, six. East returns the club jack. Should West ruff?

A good rule for defenders is not to ruff what may be one of declarer's losers. East likely would not return the jack without the ten.

If West ruffs, East will not get his diamond trick and West happens to have a trump trick anyhow.

Declarer still has to guess the hearts. But whatever he does, you are making life easier for him by your premature ruff.

DEAL 195　DISCARD PROBLEMS

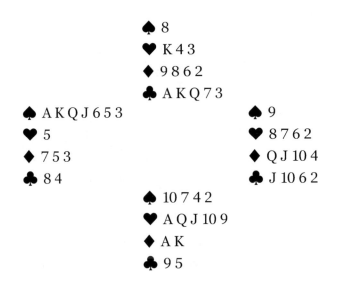

```
                        ♠ 8
                        ♥ K 4 3
                        ♦ 9 8 6 2
                        ♣ A K Q 7 3
      ♠ A K Q J 6 5 3                    ♠ 9
      ♥ 5                                ♥ 8 7 6 2
      ♦ 7 5 3                            ♦ Q J 10 4
      ♣ 8 4                              ♣ J 10 6 2
                        ♠ 10 7 4 2
                        ♥ A Q J 10 9
                        ♦ A K
                        ♣ 9 5
```

South	West	North	East
1♥	4♠	5♥	P
6♥		All Pass	

Opening Lead:　♠ King

At one table, West led the A-K of spades. Declarer ruffed the second spade with the heart king. East, staring at dummy's clubs, did not want to discard a club so he discarded a diamond.

Declarer cashed the A-K of diamonds, went to dummy with a club, and ruffed a diamond. He drew trumps and went back to dummy with his last club, discarding his three spade losers on the K-Q of clubs and the good diamond.

At the other table, the slam failed. What happened?

Sitting East at the other table was the great columnist and expert Frank Stewart who showed me this hand. The title at the top of the page is a trick question. We are talking about trumps, right?

Frank realized he could not afford to discard either minor. At Trick 2, he simply underruffed, discarding a heart, a card he couldn't possibly need.

The slam was unmakeable. Nice play Frank!

DEAL 196 · TRUMP ECHO

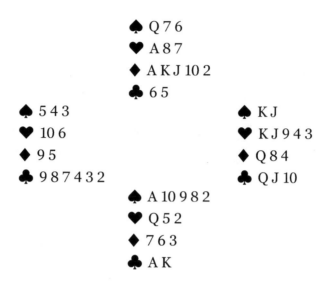

```
                    ♠ Q 7 6
                    ♥ A 8 7
                    ♦ A K J 10 2
                    ♣ 6 5
        ♠ 5 4 3                      ♠ K J
        ♥ 10 6                       ♥ K J 9 4 3
        ♦ 9 5                        ♦ Q 8 4
        ♣ 9 8 7 4 3 2                ♣ Q J 10
                    ♠ A 10 9 8 2
                    ♥ Q 5 2
                    ♦ 7 6 3
                    ♣ A K
```

East	South	West	North
1♥	1♠	P	2♥
P	2♠	P	4♠
All Pass			

Opening Lead: ♥ 10

Declarer plays low at Trick 1, East wins the king. Hoping to give West a ruff, she returns a low heart. South plays low, West the six, dummy's ace wins.

Declarer leads the spade six, jack, declarer wins the ace, West follows. South leads another spade, West follows, East wins the king.

Now what? Try to give West a heart ruff, or play the club queen?

The question is does West have another spade? How can East tell? West is supposed to give count in the trump suit, playing high-low with an odd number and low-high with an even number.

This is called Trump Echo and is just the opposite from standard count.

Of course, this requires your partner to pay attention. On this hand, West has played the five, then the three. So that means she started with an odd number.

So East can give West a heart ruff.

215

DEAL 197   TRUMP ECHO PLUS

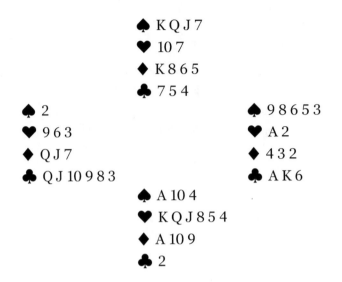

```
                    ♠ K Q J 7
                    ♥ 10 7
                    ♦ K 8 6 5
                    ♣ 7 5 4
      ♠ 2                          ♠ 9 8 6 5 3
      ♥ 9 6 3                      ♥ A 2
      ♦ Q J 7                      ♦ 4 3 2
      ♣ Q J 10 9 8 3               ♣ A K 6
                    ♠ A 10 4
                    ♥ K Q J 8 5 4
                    ♦ A 10 9
                    ♣ 2
```

South	North
1♥	1♠
3♥	4♥
P	

Opening Lead: ♠ 2

East is pretty sure that the two of spades is a singleton, not three small.

Declarer wins and leads a heart to the ten.

Which heart should West play on this first heart trick?   Why?

Not the three. West has to start a Trump Echo, a high-low to tell East he has an odd number. East wins the ace and returns a low spade, suit preference for clubs.

West ruffs with a lower trump than whatever he played the first time.

East knows West still has one more trump. After the club return, East knows he can give West another spade ruff.

DEAL 198 FIND THE SETTING TRICK

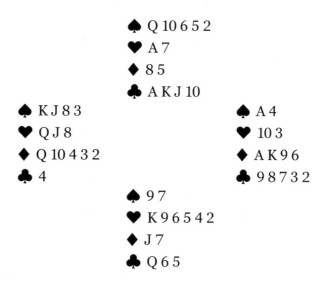

♠ Q 10 6 5 2
♥ A 7
♦ 8 5
♣ A K J 10

♠ K J 8 3
♥ Q J 8
♦ Q 10 4 3 2
♣ 4

♠ A 4
♥ 10 3
♦ A K 9 6
♣ 9 8 7 3 2

♠ 9 7
♥ K 9 6 5 4 2
♦ J 7
♣ Q 6 5

North	South
1♠	1NT
2♣	2♥
P	

Opening Lead: ♦ 3

East cashes the A-K of diamonds, West following with the two. It's unlikely West started with a doubleton diamond; that would give South five diamonds and six hearts.

So West plays ace and a spade to West's king. West continues with a third spade.

What should East play?

The highest heart he can, the ten. The defense has run out of side tricks, so it's time to see about some trump tricks. The ten does the job.

Declarer has to overruff with the king and now West has two trump tricks instead of one. That heart eight grew up. Down one.

217

DEAL 199   GROW UP

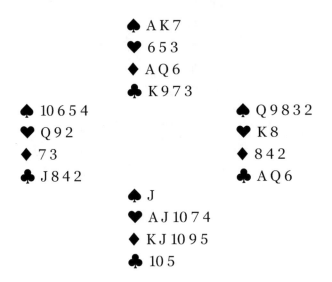

```
                    ♠ A K 7
                    ♥ 6 5 3
                    ♦ A Q 6
                    ♣ K 9 7 3
      ♠ 10 6 5 4                    ♠ Q 9 8 3 2
      ♥ Q 9 2                       ♥ K 8
      ♦ 7 3                         ♦ 8 4 2
      ♣ J 8 4 2                     ♣ A Q 6
                    ♠ J
                    ♥ A J 10 7 4
                    ♦ K J 10 9 5
                    ♣ 10 5
```

Contract: 4 ♥

Opening Lead: ♣ 2

East won the first trick with the queen. East's only hope, other than her two club tricks, had to be in trumps.

So she cashed the club ace and played a third club to dummy.

Declarer led a trump to his jack. West won the queen and returned the last club. East ruffed with the king.

When South overruffed with the ace, the nine of hearts had grown to become the setting trick.

DEAL 200 RUFF OR DON'T RUFF?

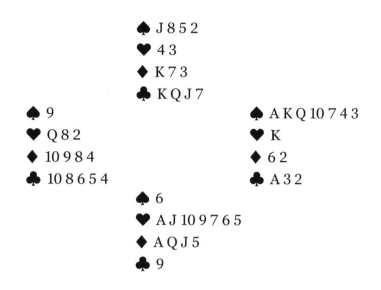

♠ J 8 5 2
♥ 4 3
♦ K 7 3
♣ K Q J 7

♠ 9
♥ Q 8 2
♦ 10 9 8 4
♣ 10 8 6 5 4

♠ A K Q 10 7 4 3
♥ K
♦ 6 2
♣ A 3 2

♠ 6
♥ A J 10 9 7 6 5
♦ A Q J 5
♣ 9

East	South	West	North
1♠	2♥	P	2NT
3♠	4♥	All Pass	

Opening Lead: ♠ 9

East won the opening lead with the spade ten and returned a suit preference queen. Declarer ruffed with the jack of trumps and West overruffed with the queen. He returned a club and East led another spade.

Declarer ruffed with the heart ten. He led the trump ace and the hand was over, making four hearts.

How would you have defended? Another declarer went down one.

The defense started the same, but when the declarer ruffed with the jack at Trick 2, West discarded instead of ruffing with a natural trump trick. The declarer led the trump ace, dropping the king and continued with the ten.

East won the queen and played a club. East led another high spade. The heart eight was now the setting trick.

DEAL 201   FIRST THINGS FIRST

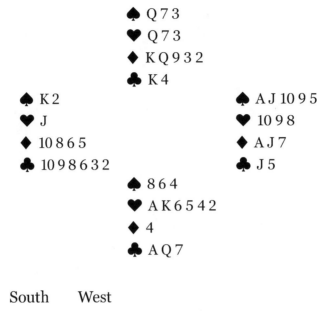

```
                    ♠ Q 7 3
                    ♥ Q 7 3
                    ♦ K Q 9 3 2
                    ♣ K 4
      ♠ K 2                           ♠ A J 10 9 5
      ♥ J                             ♥ 10 9 8
      ♦ 10 8 6 5                      ♦ A J 7
      ♣ 10 9 8 6 3 2                  ♣ J 5
                    ♠ 8 6 4
                    ♥ A K 6 5 4 2
                    ♦ 4
                    ♣ A Q 7
```

North	East	South	West
1♦	1♠	2♥	P
3♥	All Pass		

Opening Lead: ♠ King

South did well to stop at three hearts. Even that turned out to be too high when E/W defended accurately. West led the spade king, then the spade two.

West won the ten, then cashed the spade ace.

How should East defend from this point?

If East carelessly leads another spade for a trump promotion, declarer will counter by just discarding his diamond loser. The defenders will promote a trump trick, but that's all.

A helpful rule of defensive play is cashing your side suit winners, in this case the diamond ace, before trying for the trump promotion.

If East defends properly, South has no counter. After the diamond ace and another spade, the heart jack promotes East's trump holding. Down one.

DEAL 202   REMEMBER?

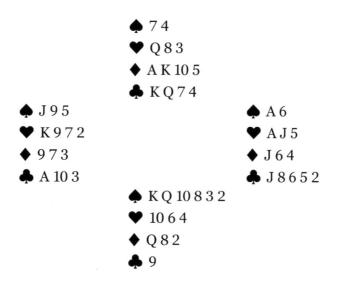

```
              ♠ 7 4
              ♥ Q 8 3
              ♦ A K 10 5
              ♣ K Q 7 4
♠ J 9 5                      ♠ A 6
♥ K 9 7 2                    ♥ A J 5
♦ 9 7 3                      ♦ J 6 4
♣ A 10 3                     ♣ J 8 6 5 2
              ♠ K Q 10 8 3 2
              ♥ 10 6 4
              ♦ Q 8 2
              ♣ 9
```

North	South
1♣	1♠
1NT	2♠
P	

Opening Lead: ♥ 2

West led the heart two, East winning the jack. East cashed the heart ace and returned his last heart to West's king.

Like the previous hand, If West plays the last heart, East can (must) ruff with the spade ace, promoting West's spade jack into the setting trick.

But only if?

Exactly. West must cash the club ace first, otherwise, declarer can throw a loser, the club nine, while the defenders are enjoying their promotion.

DEAL 203   KNOCK, KNOCK

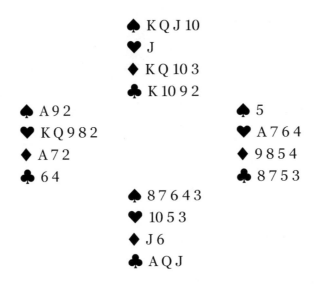

```
                    ♠ K Q J 10
                    ♥ J
                    ♦ K Q 10 3
                    ♣ K 10 9 2
    ♠ A 9 2                         ♠ 5
    ♥ K Q 9 8 2                     ♥ A 7 6 4
    ♦ A 7 2                         ♦ 9 8 5 4
    ♣ 6 4                           ♣ 8 7 5 3
                    ♠ 8 7 6 4 3
                    ♥ 10 5 3
                    ♦ J 6
                    ♣ A Q J
```

West	North	East	South
1♥	Dbl	3♥	3♠
P	4♠		All Pass

Opening Lead: ♥ King

West holds the first trick with the king. It's obvious that South's spades are weak.

Most "tapping" or shortening defenses involve attacking the declarer's trump holding.

But here West can see the obvious defense. Play another heart now making dummy ruff with an honor.

West will be regaining the lead with an ace to make dummy ruff again. Once dummy has used two honors, West's nine of spades will be the setting trick.

DEAL 204   WHERE YOU FIND IT

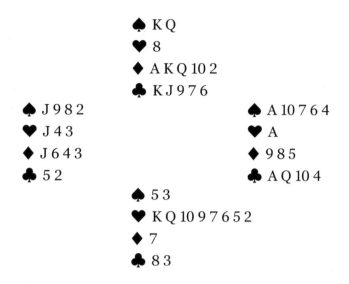

♠ K Q
♥ 8
♦ A K Q 10 2
♣ K J 9 7 6

♠ J 9 8 2
♥ J 4 3
♦ J 6 4 3
♣ 5 2

♠ A 10 7 6 4
♥ A
♦ 9 8 5
♣ A Q 10 4

♠ 5 3
♥ K Q 10 9 7 6 5 2
♦ 7
♣ 8 3

North	East	South	West
1♦	1♠	4♥	All Pass

Opening Lead: ♠ 2

East won the opening lead. Seeing three tricks, where was the fourth? A spade ruff seemed unlikely, but he returned an unimaginative spade. Declarer lost three aces, making four hearts.

Too bad West didn't lead a club.

Could you have found a fourth trick?

Remember when there seems to be no hope, look to the trump suit, even though it might seem unlikely.

The defender at the other table, seeing those diamonds, and thinking ahead, cashed the club ace and played another club.

When he got in with the trump ace, he played a third club and Voila! Partner's jack of trumps was the setting trick!

He who looks finds.

DEAL 205   CAREFUL

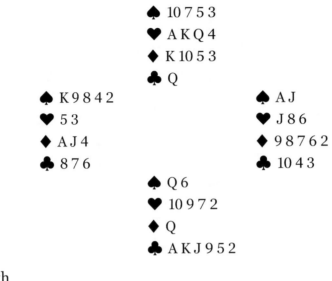

♠ 10 7 5 3
♥ A K Q 4
♦ K 10 5 3
♣ Q

♠ K 9 8 4 2
♥ 5 3
♦ A J 4
♣ 8 7 6

♠ A J
♥ J 8 6
♦ 9 8 7 6 2
♣ 10 4 3

♠ Q 6
♥ 10 9 7 2
♦ Q
♣ A K J 9 5 2

North	South
1♦	2♣
2NT	3♥
4♥	P

Opening Lead: ♠ 4

East won the ace and returned the jack, declarer the queen, West the king.

:   How should West continue the defense from here?

At one table, West played the ♠9 from his ♠982. East ruffed with the heart six, declarer overruffed, drew trumps and made an overtrick.

Who would you blame for this defense?

The yelling started. West said, "Ruff the third spade with your heart jack, partner. You know declarer is out, too." East thought, then yelled back, "Cash your diamond ace first, otherwise, declarer will just discard his diamond loser."

Usually he who yells first is wrong. Here both East and West contributed to the poor defense.

DEAL 206   OPTIONS

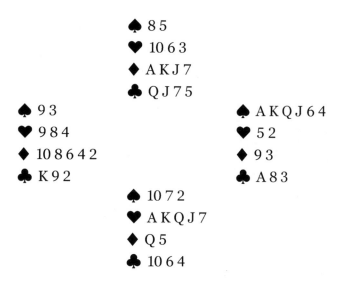

```
                        ♠ 8 5
                        ♥ 10 6 3
                        ♦ A K J 7
                        ♣ Q J 7 5
         ♠ 9 3                          ♠ A K Q J 6 4
         ♥ 9 8 4                        ♥ 5 2
         ♦ 10 8 6 4 2                   ♦ 9 3
         ♣ K 9 2                        ♣ A 8 3
                        ♠ 10 7 2
                        ♥ A K Q J 7
                        ♦ Q 5
                        ♣ 10 6 4
```

South	West	North	East
1♥	P	1NT	2♠
P	P	4♥	All Pass

Opening Lead: ♠ 9

East wins the first two tricks, West following with the spade three. If West holds the ♥ J x x or ♥ Q x, another spade will promote a trump trick for you.

What should East play at Trick 3? Maybe "ask" West.

A trump promotion might be right or not. Play the club ace and West should tell you what to do.

On the club ace, West plays the nine.

Do you think he wants a trump promotion or a club?

DEAL 207　WHO IS TO BLAME?

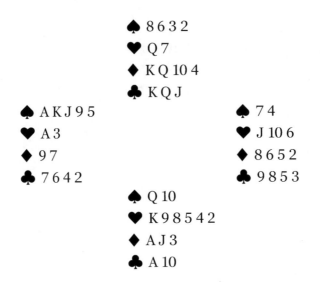

♠ 8 6 3 2
♥ Q 7
♦ K Q 10 4
♣ K Q J

♠ A K J 9 5
♥ A 3
♦ 9 7
♣ 7 6 4 2

♠ 7 4
♥ J 10 6
♦ 8 6 5 2
♣ 9 8 5 3

♠ Q 10
♥ K 9 8 5 4 2
♦ A J 3
♣ A 10

South	West	North	East
1♥	1♠	2♦	P
2♥	P	4♥	All Pass

Opening Lead:　♠ Ace

West led the A-K of spades and continued with the jack. East discarded a club at Trick 3, South ruffing. Declarer played a trump to the queen and returned a trump. East followed with the ten and declarer ducked, losing to West's ace.

Declarer took the rest, making four hearts.

How could the defense have done better? Assign the blame.
How about 80% East, 20% West? Why?

East should ruff the third spade with the heart ten; it can't hurt and might help. South will overruff with the king. But now when South leads a trump, West can rise with the ace. East's jack is the setting trick.

Why 20% West? Maybe foreseeing the whole hand, West could force East to do the right thing by leading a low spade, not the jack, to force East to ruff, high we hope. Hey, partners need help.

226

DEAL 208   A LITTLE FANCY DANCING

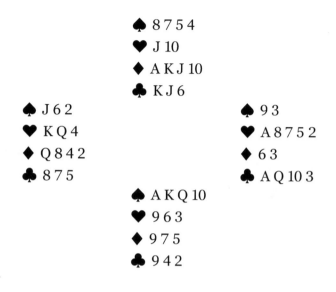

```
                    ♠ 8 7 5 4
                    ♥ J 10
                    ♦ A K J 10
                    ♣ K J 6
        ♠ J 6 2                    ♠ 9 3
        ♥ K Q 4                    ♥ A 8 7 5 2
        ♦ Q 8 4 2                  ♦ 6 3
        ♣ 8 7 5                    ♣ A Q 10 3
                    ♠ A K Q 10
                    ♥ 9 6 3
                    ♦ 9 7 5
                    ♣ 9 4 2
```

North	East	South	West
1♦	1♥	1♠	2♥
2♠	All Pass		

Opening Lead: ♥ King

East should play a discouraging two at Trick 1. West will make the obvious switch to a club. Declarer plays the jack, East winning the queen.

How should East continue?

East can now underlead her heart ace to West for another club play. East wins the ten and cashes the ace.

Seeing no more defensive tricks, she can lead the thirteenth club.

West now has a trump trick. Down one.

DEAL 209   DESPERATE TIMES

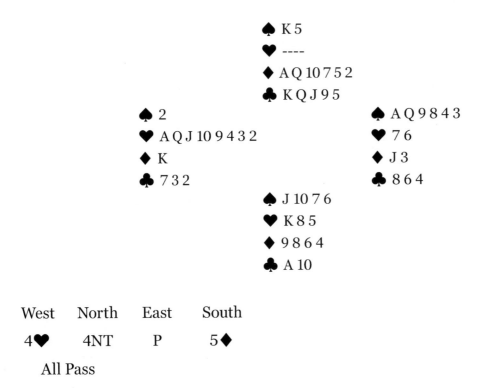

```
                    ♠ K 5
                    ♥ ----
                    ♦ A Q 10 7 5 2
                    ♣ K Q J 9 5
        ♠ 2                         ♠ A Q 9 8 4 3
        ♥ A Q J 10 9 4 3 2         ♥ 7 6
        ♦ K                         ♦ J 3
        ♣ 7 3 2                     ♣ 8 6 4
                    ♠ J 10 7 6
                    ♥ K 8 5
                    ♦ 9 8 6 4
                    ♣ A 10
```

West	North	East	South
4♥	4NT	P	5♦
	All Pass		

Opening Lead: ♠ 2

West opening preempt is swept aside as the opponents reach five diamonds after North's Unusual No Trump takeout.

How should East defend?

It looks grim. East wins the first two tricks, West showing out on the second spade. Where is another trick coming from?

What card do you need from partner? If he has the ace of clubs (unlikely), it's not going away.

But what else? Yes, try another spade. A good partner will have the diamond king! Your diamond jack just grew up.

DEAL 210   MORE DESPERATE MEASURES

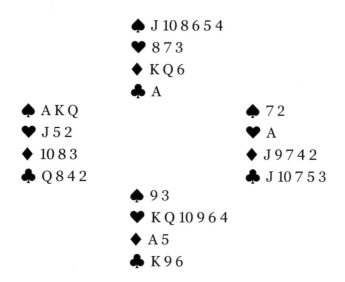

Contract: 4 ♥

Opening Lead: ♠ Ace

Declarer ruffed the third spade. She played a club to dummy and led a heart.

After East won the ace, the hand was over.

Could the defense have done better?

Yes. Trump promotions can be very obscure.

East can see after the A-K of spades takes two tricks that there are probably no other defensive tricks coming except trumps.

If East ruffs the spade queen with the ace of trumps, South goes down. West's jack of hearts is the setting trick.

DEAL 211   LITTLE THINGS MEAN A LOT

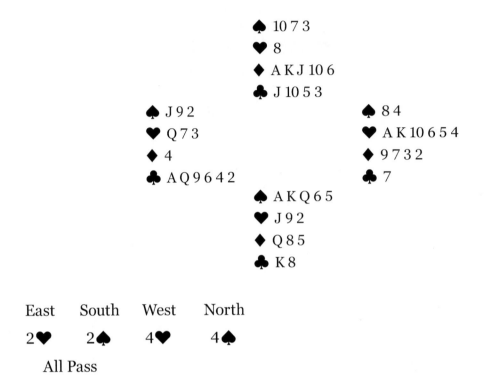

♠ 10 7 3
♥ 8
♦ A K J 10 6
♣ J 10 5 3

♠ J 9 2
♥ Q 7 3
♦ 4
♣ A Q 9 6 4 2

♠ 8 4
♥ A K 10 6 5 4
♦ 9 7 3 2
♣ 7

♠ A K Q 6 5
♥ J 9 2
♦ Q 8 5
♣ K 8

East	South	West	North
2♥	2♠	4♥	4♠
All Pass			

Opening Lead: ♥ 3

East wins the first trick and switches to his singleton club. Declarer plays low, West wins the queen, then the ace, and continues with another club.

Who is going to prevail, the offense or the defense?

The fate of the contract lies with East. He obviously is going to ruff the club, unaware South has no more clubs either.

At one table, East ruffed with the four and declarer overruffed with the five. Declarer drew trumps and claimed.

At another table, East ruffed with the eight. Voila, look what happened! Declarer overruffed, of course, but with the queen. Now it was West claiming for down one, showing declarer his three trumps to the now high jack.

How did you do?

DEAL 212   NOT ALWAYS BEST

So now that we have reviewed and become experts at defending with trump promotion. Of course it's not always right even when it looks so obvious.

From the "Bridge Bulletin" September, 2019, Mike Lawrence showed:

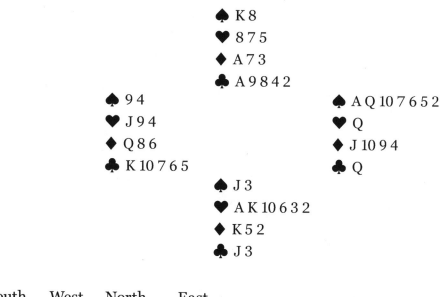

```
                    ♠ K 8
                    ♥ 8 7 5
                    ♦ A 7 3
                    ♣ A 9 8 4 2
      ♠ 9 4                        ♠ A Q 10 7 6 5 2
      ♥ J 9 4                      ♥ Q
      ♦ Q 8 6                      ♦ J 10 9 4
      ♣ K 10 7 6 5                 ♣ Q
                    ♠ J 3
                    ♥ A K 10 6 3 2
                    ♦ K 5 2
                    ♣ J 3
```

South	West	North	East
1♥	P	2♣	3♠
P	P	4♥	All Pass

Opening Lead: ♠ 9

East took the first two tricks and considered how to continue. Meanwhile South was thinking "I've lost two tricks already, I have a club and diamond loser, and hearts are probably not 2/2. I'm going down at least two."

Without seeing all four hands, consider East's problem. A safe heart or diamond exit? The singleton club? But having read my book, he opted for a trump promotion and played a spade.

South discarded a club, West ruffed with the heart nine, and declarer discarded a diamond from dummy.

Now being able to ruff a diamond in dummy, the defense heard those dreaded words, "I claim." He had ten tricks with one ruff.

DEAL 213   OVERRUFF? YES OR NO?

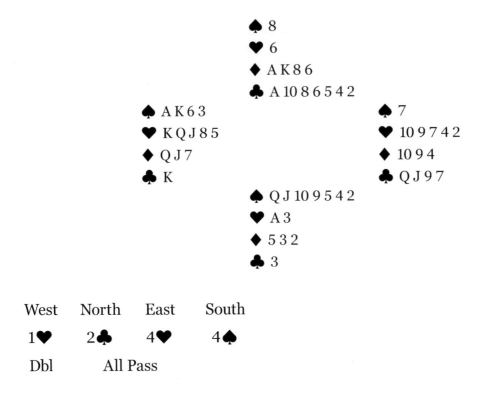

```
                    ♠ 8
                    ♥ 6
                    ♦ A K 8 6
                    ♣ A 10 8 6 5 4 2
   ♠ A K 6 3                          ♠ 7
   ♥ K Q J 8 5                        ♥ 10 9 7 4 2
   ♦ Q J 7                            ♦ 10 9 4
   ♣ K                                ♣ Q J 9 7
                    ♠ Q J 10 9 5 4 2
                    ♥ A 3
                    ♦ 5 3 2
                    ♣ 3
```

West	North	East	South
1♥	2♣	4♥	4♠
Dbl		All Pass	

Opening Lead: ♥ King

Declarer wins the ace and ruffs a heart (maybe West should have led a trump?). Declarer plays the club ace and ruffs a club with the spade queen.

How should West continue?

Please don't tell me you overruffed. A good rule is only overruff with useless trumps, not tricks you were getting anyhow. Watch.

If you overruffed, declarer will be able to draw trumps, losing one more trump and a diamond. If you discarded, watch the spots. South's jack loses to your ace. His ten loses to your king. His nine takes your three. But now your six is higher than his five!

Could declarer have played in a differently manner? Not your problem.

DEAL 214   WHO GROWS UP

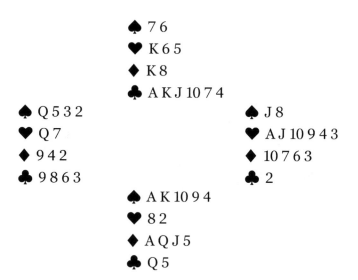

```
                  ♠ 7 6
                  ♥ K 6 5
                  ♦ K 8
                  ♣ A K J 10 7 4
    ♠ Q 5 3 2                    ♠ J 8
    ♥ Q 7                        ♥ A J 10 9 4 3
    ♦ 9 4 2                      ♦ 10 7 6 3
    ♣ 9 8 6 3                    ♣ 2
                  ♠ A K 10 9 4
                  ♥ 8 2
                  ♦ A Q J 5
                  ♣ Q 5
```

North	East	South	West
1♣	2♥	2♠	P
3♣	P	4♦	P
4♠	All Pass		

Opening Lead: ♥ Queen

The defense started with three rounds of hearts. Declarer ruffed the third round with the spade ten but West overruffed with the spade queen.

West returned a club. Declarer cashed the A-K of trumps. When the jack fell, declarer drew the last trump and claimed.

How did the defense prevail at another table?

The defense started the same but at Trick 3, instead of overruffing with a trick she was getting anyhow, West discarded a diamond. Declarer next took the A-K of trumps, drawing East's ♠J but crashing the ♠76 in dummy.

Now West had the ♠Q5 behind declarer's ♠94. The spade five was going to be the setting trick. Maybe not what West envisioned when she first picked up her hand.

The little guy had grown up.

DEAL 215   WISHFUL THINKING DOESN'T TAKE MUCH

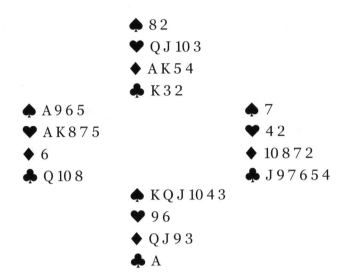

```
                        ♠ 8 2
                        ♥ Q J 10 3
                        ♦ A K 5 4
                        ♣ K 3 2
        ♠ A 9 6 5                      ♠ 7
        ♥ A K 8 7 5                    ♥ 4 2
        ♦ 6                            ♦ 10 8 7 2
        ♣ Q 10 8                       ♣ J 9 7 6 5 4
                        ♠ K Q J 10 4 3
                        ♥ 9 6
                        ♦ Q J 9 3
                        ♣ A
```

West	North	East	South
1♥	P	P	2♠
P	3NT	P	4♠
All Pass			

Opening Lead: ♥ Ace

At Trick 1, East plays the heart four, declarer the nine. West has to consider how to proceed. Is the heart king cashing?

The missing hearts are the two and six. If declarer has a singleton, would East play the four from ♥942 ? OK, so the king is cashing.

That's two tricks and the ace of trumps the third.

Can West imagine a layout where he might win another trick?

The minors look grim. What about the spade nine? What would you need from East? Not much.

Play another heart. East ruffs with the seven. Just what the doctor ordered. Declarer overruffs with the ten and now?

Right. Down one, West scoring the spade nine.

DEAL 216   DON'T GET ENDPLAYED

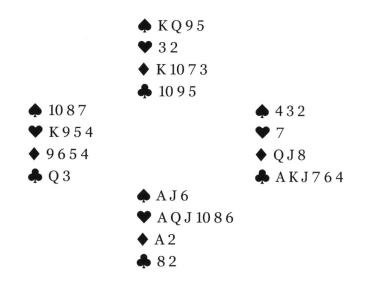

♠ K Q 9 5
♥ 3 2
♦ K 10 7 3
♣ 10 9 5

♠ 10 8 7   ♠ 4 3 2
♥ K 9 5 4   ♥ 7
♦ 9 6 5 4   ♦ Q J 8
♣ Q 3   ♣ A K J 7 6 4

♠ A J 6
♥ A Q J 10 8 6
♦ A 2
♣ 8 2

Contract: 4 ♥ (East overcalls in ♣'s)
Opening Lead: ♣ Queen

East won the first two club tricks and continued with the club jack. Declarer ruffed with the heart queen. West overruffed with the king. Declarer won the return, drew the remaining trumps and claimed. Making four hearts.

How would you have defended as West? Is not overruffing all there is?

At the other table, West realized by not overruffing she could score two trump tricks. Instead, she discarded, a good play, but a diamond. (What would you have discarded?) Declarer now played the A-K of diamonds and ruffed a diamond. He then cashed three rounds of spades.

With four cards to be played, West held ♥K954, declarer ♥AJ108. South played the ♥J. Whether West won this trick or the next, she was trump endplayed and could only score one trump trick. What happened?

On the third club, West had to discard a spade, not a diamond, to avoid this endplay. Then she could have ruffed the third spade and exited a heart.

Thanks to Mike Lawrence for this most interesting hand.

DEAL 217   FALSE COUNT

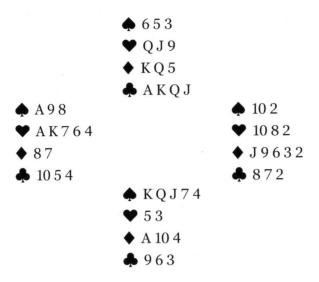

♠ 6 5 3
♥ Q J 9
♦ K Q 5
♣ A K Q J

♠ A 9 8
♥ A K 7 6 4
♦ 8 7
♣ 10 5 4

♠ 10 2
♥ 10 8 2
♦ J 9 6 3 2
♣ 8 7 2

♠ K Q J 7 4
♥ 5 3
♦ A 10 4
♣ 9 6 3

North	South	
1♣	1♠	
2NT	3♦*	New Minor
3♠	4♠	
P		

Opening Lead: ♥ Ace

East, not wanting a switch, and maybe with some foresight, played the heart ten at Trick 1. West continued with the king and another, expecting to give East a heart ruff. She was annoyed when her husband followed to the third heart.

Why did West's mood change as the hand progressed?

Declarer led a spade to the king. West won the ace and played another heart. East ruffed with the ten of spades and when declarer overruffed, West had a second trump trick.

"Nice play of the heart ten," West begrudgingly said to her husband.
"Just trying to help steer you in the right direction, dear."

DEAL 218   DELICATE DISCARDING

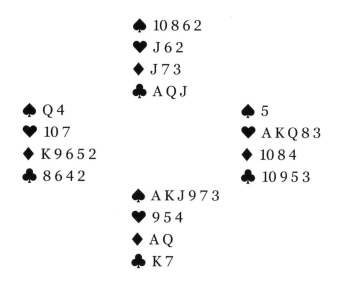

```
                    ♠ 10 8 6 2
                    ♥ J 6 2
                    ♦ J 7 3
                    ♣ A Q J
     ♠ Q 4                          ♠ 5
     ♥ 10 7                         ♥ A K Q 8 3
     ♦ K 9 6 5 2                    ♦ 10 8 4
     ♣ 8 6 4 2                      ♣ 10 9 5 3
                    ♠ A K J 9 7 3
                    ♥ 9 5 4
                    ♦ A Q
                    ♣ K 7
```

South   North

1♠   2♠

4♠   P

Opening Lead: ♥ 10

West guesses to lead a heart. East cashes the A-K-Q, declarer following. West has to discard on the third round. He threw the diamond nine.

At Trick 4, East obeyed and shifted to a diamond. Declarer won the ace, drew trumps, and threw his diamond loser on the long club.

What would you have discarded?

If partner has the club king, he is probably getting it. But holding the Q 4 of trumps, you know that another round of hearts will give you a trump promotion.

Discard the two of diamonds. If he still persists with a diamond, tell him to check your convention card. Ask him when you switched to upside-down carding?

DEAL 219   TAPPING DEFENSE, BUT TAP WHO?

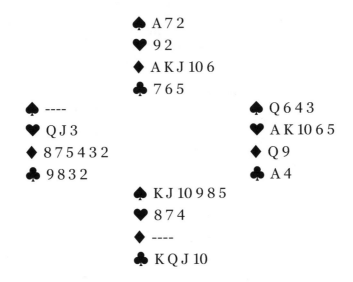

```
                    ♠ A 7 2
                    ♥ 9 2
                    ♦ A K J 10 6
                    ♣ 7 6 5
     ♠ ----                      ♠ Q 6 4 3
     ♥ Q J 3                     ♥ A K 10 6 5
     ♦ 8 7 5 4 3 2               ♦ Q 9
     ♣ 9 8 3 2                   ♣ A 4
                    ♠ K J 10 9 8 5
                    ♥ 8 7 4
                    ♦ ----
                    ♣ K Q J 10
```

Contract: 4 ♠

Opening Lead: ♥ Queen

East is counting his defensive prospects. There are probably two hearts, one diamond, and a possible spade. He played an encouraging ♥10. West continued with the ♥J, East followed with the ♥6. West shifted to a high club. East won the ♣A and returned a club, declarer winning the ♣K.

Declarer won and led to the ♠A, carefully unblocking the ♠8 from his hand. This terrific play was rewarded when West showed out.

Now he could lead the ♠7 for a finesse and stay in the dummy, having the ♠5 in his hand. Making four spades.

How could the defense have prevailed? Whose fault was this>

Declarer made a wonderful unblocking play, but East should take over the defense at Trick 2. Overtake the ♥J and make dummy ruff a high heart.

Declarer can no longer pick up his ♠Q. Down one.

DEAL 220   OPENING LEAD

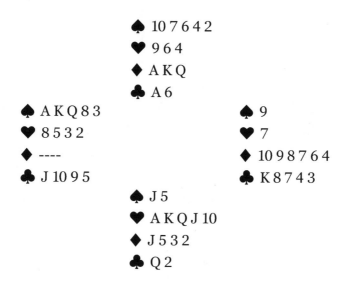

```
                    ♠ 10 7 6 4 2
                    ♥ 9 6 4
                    ♦ A K Q
                    ♣ A 6
   ♠ A K Q 8 3                        ♠ 9
   ♥ 8 5 3 2                          ♥ 7
   ♦ ----                            ♦ 10 9 8 7 6 4
   ♣ J 10 9 5                        ♣ K 8 7 4 3
                    ♠ J 5
                    ♥ A K Q J 10
                    ♦ J 5 3 2
                    ♣ Q 2
```

South	West	North	East
1♥	1♠	2♠	P
3♥	P	4♥	All Pass

Opening Lead: ♠ King (E/W agreement is Ace from A-K)

West leads the spade king, then the spade ace.

What should East play at Trick 2? Low club? Low diamond? Other?

It better be "other" What other?

When the opening lead is the king, then the ace in a bid suit, so not a doubleton, and your normal agreement is ace from A-K, what does that mean?

It means "I can ruff something." So "other" is to ruff your partner's ace and return your longest suit, diamonds, the four, suit preference for clubs.

Down one, you win a club in the end. Nice play!

239

DEAL 221 WHEN

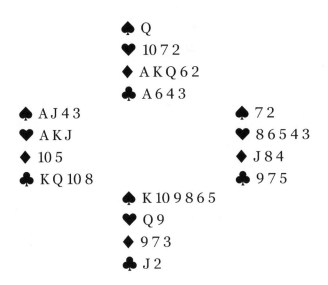

```
                    ♠ Q
                    ♥ 10 7 2
                    ♦ A K Q 6 2
                    ♣ A 6 4 3
    ♠ A J 4 3                    ♠ 7 2
    ♥ A K J                      ♥ 8 6 5 4 3
    ♦ 10 5                       ♦ J 8 4
    ♣ K Q 10 8                   ♣ 9 7 5
                    ♠ K 10 9 8 6 5
                    ♥ Q 9
                    ♦ 9 7 3
                    ♣ J 2
```

North	East	South	West
1♦	P	1♠	Dbl
1NT	P	2♠	All Pass

Opening Lead: ♥ Ace

West led the heart ace, East played the three and West continued with the club king. Declarer won and played the spade queen.

Should West take this trick? What is West's defensive plan?

West sees two spades, two hearts, and one club. Perhaps if he can make South ruff enough times, he can take a trick with his last spade. There is no rush to win this first spade trick. Declarer has to return to his hand.

Say South gives West his club trick. West can continue clubs, making South ruff.

South gives West a spade. West makes South ruff another club. West gets in with another spade and plays the heart king and jack. South ruffs with his last trump, but West still has a spade. Down one.

If West takes the first spade, South has the timing to draw all the trumps and use all dummy's diamonds, instead of West ruffing the last diamond.

240

Printed in the United States
by Baker & Taylor Publisher Services